"Paul Feider's newest book, *Experience the Healing Miracles of Jesus*, gives us a unique experience. He invites us to 'come and see' Jesus. Even though we may know these miracles of Jesus from the Bible, Feider gives a new perspective into them. With in-depth reflections intertwined with personal stories, he takes us to another level of understanding Jesus. It is truly an enjoyable journey."

—VICKIE BAUCH, convener, Order of St. Luke,

"*Experience the Healing Miracles of Jesus* gives me the fuel and the fire to continue to learn, apply, and participate in bringing the healing energy of Jesus to all God's people. Divine love heals, and we are called to be open to Jesus's power to heal. This book is an excellent training tool to walk us through the miracles showing us why and how Jesus healed. Feider takes us deeper by showing us that the ultimate goal is to draw us into a committed faith relationship with God. Our role is to bring the fullness of life in Christ to all."

—LYDIA SWALCHICK, coordinator, ACT Conference

"As pilgrims, we journey with Jesus, desiring to be made whole. Paul Feider's book, *Experience the Healing Miracles of Jesus*, helps us connect deeply with Jesus through his healing ministry. This biblical, reflective, and practical devotional encourages and challenges readers to engage with contemporary healing ministry. For those unsure, I highly recommend reading this book. For those already familiar, it's a must-read."

—TODD A. MCGREGOR, founder, Diocese of Toliara, Madagascar

"With great wisdom and grace, Paul Feider opens the door and invites us into a journey of Jesus's healing ministry in his book, *Experience the Healing Miracles of Jesus*. It is a journey rooted in the healing power of God's love. It is a journey that will draw the reader into a deeper understanding of the many ways Jesus prayed healing for body, mind, and spirit. It is a journey where we will discover that we can and are being empowered by the Holy Spirit and equipped by Jesus himself, to be his loving and healing presence to God's people in the world today."

—JOHN RICE, director, The Blessing Place, North Carolina

"As a teacher of the OSL Foundational Study, *The Healing Miracles of Jesus*, I very much appreciate this new work by Paul Feider, *Experience the Healing Miracles of Jesus*. In this well-researched and thoughtful exposition of twenty-nine unique healing accounts from the gospels, Feider provides rich insight and commentary. The depth of reflection offered for each unique account is unparalleled and compelling, and Feider uses examples from his lifelong healing ministry to illustrate these accounts. Feider also poses thought provoking questions and exercises at the end of each reflection to draw the reader into practical application spurred by each account. I plan to use this book as a reference text alongside the handbook in our 26 Miracles Prayer Minister Training Course."

—MIKE SABBACK, convener, OSL South Carolina

"I just finished reading *Experience the Healing Miracles of Jesus*, and I say excellent!!! I could not put this book down and I was not ready for it to be over when I finished reading the last page. Everyone who is new to the healing ministry or has been in the ministry for years needs to read this book. Paul Feider invites the reader into each of the healing miracles of Jesus and unpacks them for use as a model when doing healing prayer ministry. This book is filled with Feider's years of wisdom in preaching, teaching, and working with pioneers in the healing ministry such as Francis and Judith MacNutt, Craig Miller, John Rice, and many others. It's practical, it's scriptural, and it's a wonderful resource. Thank you, Fr. Paul. This is your best work yet!"
—TAMILA HENNESSY, regional coordinator, ACTheals

"In this book, Paul Feider digs into details about each of the healings of Jesus's ministry. His insight documents both the truth and the mystery of Jesus's healings. Each of us, as we travel the path of faith, need encouragement and excitement to keep moving us along. The subtitle of the book, *A Journey into the Mystery*, is an excellent description of where Feider wants us to go. Mystery is that exciting part of Jesus's ministry that energizes us, that keeps us looking for more, that keeps us engaged, that makes it personal. As we unwrap this mystery of healing, we move closer to a personal relationship with Jesus, and therefore closer to God the Father. This book will reignite your quest to go on a discovery trip to unwrap some of the mysteries of faith. A must read if you are interested at all about the mysteries of God's love for you today."
—KEN KURTENACKER, disciple

Experience the Healing Miracles of Jesus

Experience the Healing Miracles of Jesus

A Journey into the Mystery

PAUL FEIDER

RESOURCE *Publications* • Eugene, Oregon

EXPERIENCE THE HEALING MIRACLES OF JESUS
A Journey into the Mystery

Copyright © 2025 Paul Feider. All rights reserved. Except for brief quotations in critical publications or reviews, no part of this book may be reproduced in any manner without prior written permission from the publisher. Write: Permissions, Wipf and Stock Publishers, 199 W. 8th Ave., Suite 3, Eugene, OR 97401.

Resource Publications
An Imprint of Wipf and Stock Publishers
199 W. 8th Ave., Suite 3
Eugene, OR 97401

www.wipfandstock.com

PAPERBACK ISBN: 979-8-3852-4380-8
HARDCOVER ISBN: 979-8-3852-4381-5
EBOOK ISBN: 979-8-3852-4382-2

03/10/25

Scriptures taken from *The Holy Bible,* New International Version, NIV. Copyright 1973, 1978, 1984, 2011 by Biblica, Inc. All rights reserved worldwide.

A heart felt thank you to:

Donna Self for her marvelous job of editing,

Mike Sabback for his support and encouragement,

Vickie Bauch, Ken Kurtenacker,
and Tim and Sue Wilson for their helpful comments,

And Jesus for the inspiration and the energy to write.

Contents

Introduction	xi
Healing Account 1: The Royal Official's Son John 4:46–54	3
Healing Account 2: The Man with an Evil Spirit Mark 1:21–28 (Luke 4:31–37)	8
Healing Account 3: Simon's Mother-In-Law Mark 1:29–31 (Matthew 8:14–15 and Luke 4:38–39)	12
Healing Account 4: The Man with Leprosy Mark 1:40–45 (Matthew 8:1–4 and Luke 5:12–16)	15
Healing Account 5: The Paralytic Mark 2:1–12	19
Healing Account 6: The Woman at the Well John 4:4–17, 28–32, 39–42	24
Healing Account 7: The Man at the Pool Side John 5:1–17	31
Healing Account 8: The Man with a Shriveled Hand Mark 3:1–6 (Matthew 12:9–14 and Luke 6:6–11)	35
Healing Account 9: The Centurion's Servant Matthew 8:5–13 (Luke 7:1–10)	39
Healing Account 10: The Widow's Son Luke 7:11–17	43
Healing Account 11: The Gerasene Demoniac Mark 5:1–20 (Matthew 8:28–34 and Luke 8:26–39)	47

Contents

Healing Account 12: The Woman with a Hemorrhage — 53
  Mark 5:24b—34 (Matthew 9:20–22 and Luke 8:42–48)

Healing Account 13: Jairus's Daughter — 58
  Mark 5:21–24, 35–43 (Matthew 9:18–19, 23–26
  and Luke 8:40–42, 49–56)

Healing Account 14: Two Blind Men — 62
  Matthew 9:27–31

Healing Account 15: The Mute, Possessed Man — 65
  Matthew 9:32–34

Healing Account 16: The Daughter of the Canaanite Woman — 68
  Mark 7:24–30 (Matthew 15:21–28)

Healing Account 17: Deaf Man with a Speech Impediment — 72
  Mark 7:31–37

Healing Account 18: The Blind Man at Bethsaida — 76
  Mark 8:22–26

Healing Account 19: The Epileptic Boy — 80
  Mark 9:14–28 (Matthew 17:14–20 and Luke 9:37–43)

Healing Account 20: The Woman Caught in Adultery — 84
  John 8:1–11

Healing Account 21: The Man Born Blind — 89
  John 9:1–38

Healing Account 22: Blind, Dumb, and Possessed Man — 95
  Matthew 12:22–28 (Mark 20–27 and Luke 11:14–26)

Healing Account 23: A Crippled Woman — 100
  Luke 13:10–17

Healing Account 24: The Man with Dropsy — 104
  Luke 14:1–6

Healing Account 25: Ten Lepers — 107
  Luke 17:11–19

Healing Account 26: Zacchaeus — 110
  Luke 19:1–10

Contents

Healing Account 27: The Raising of Lazarus 115
John 11:1–46

Healing Account 28: A Blind Beggar 122
Mark 10:46–52 (Matthew 20:29–34 and Luke 18:35–43)

Healing Account 29: Malchus's Ear 126
Luke 22:47–51 (Matthew 26:50–52; Mark 14:47,
and John 18:10–11, 25–27)

The Resurrection of Jesus 129
Luke 24:1–12 (Mark 16:1–8, Matthew 28:1–10,
and John 20:1–18)

Appendix 133

About the Author 139

Books for Further Reading 141

Introduction

The gospels contain rich divine treasures that invite us into the mystery of healing and the miracles that flowed from Jesus' life. These inspired writings take us into the life of Jesus and open the way for us to do the things he did by the power of his love. The four gospels enlighten a way of living that allows us to bring healing power to our lives and those with whom we live and work. These writings contain the keys to discovering the essence of divine healing and show us how to make that power available today. This book will unlock these divine treasures and inspire you to investigate the healing ministry of Jesus so that your life can be immersed in the divine energy available to every baptized person. You can experience the healing energy of Jesus' love. Enter into this discovery journey and open yourself to the awesome mystery of Jesus' divine healing.

I invite you to walk with me into the gospels of Mark, Matthew, Luke, and John to experience the healing miracles of Jesus so that you can offer the gift of healing in every encounter you have. If you are in the healthcare field, this journey will open the way for you to augment your practice with divine energy to bring healing beyond the limits of your human skills. If you are a therapist, discovering divine healing power will allow you to go deeper into the core issues of the people you serve and release the pain of their inner wounds that you alone could not reach. If you are a healing prayer minister or pastor of a church, this search will offer new insights on how you can take people to a much greater wholeness by the power of Jesus' healing love. If you are a person who wants to learn more about how you can participate in the divine healing described in the gospels, then this journey will give you the tools to do what you desire. I welcome you to delve into the texts with me and experience the richness and the power in the divinely inspired gospels and the stories of the healing miracles.

Let me say that there are people who teach that these miracles never happened, and they even say that Jesus never rose from the dead or that he was the Son of God. They simply ignore the overwhelming evidence that these things occurred. The gospel of Mark was written only a couple of decades after the resurrection. The most plausible evidence indicates that Mark was the scribe of the apostle Peter, who saw many of the miracles with his own eyes. His was the first of the gospels written. When a healing story is in more than one gospel, I will focus on Mark's account because it was written closest to the actual happenings. The other gospel writers either saw the miracles or knew people who saw them. They were recording testimonies of eyewitnesses. They could not record these stories if they did not occur. Other people who saw the miracles were still alive when these accounts were written. These living witnesses validate the gospel stories.

Regarding the resurrection of Jesus, the apostle Paul wrote the following words to his community in Corinth. He wrote, "For what I received I passed on to you as of first importance: that Christ died for our sins according to the scriptures, that he was buried, that he was raised on the third day according to the scriptures, and that he appeared to Peter, and then to the Twelve. After that, he appeared to more than five hundred of the brothers at the same time, most of whom are still living, though some have fallen asleep. Then he appeared to James, then to all the apostles, and last of all he appeared to me also, as to one abnormally born" (1 Corinthians 15:3–8). Paul could not write these things for public reading if they were not true since there were people who were still alive who saw Jesus alive after the resurrection. The gospels also attest to Jesus' resurrection and that he was the Son of God. The very fact that so many people changed their lives and experienced Jesus as alive confirms this report. J. P. Moreland makes a convincing case

Introduction

for the reliability of these accounts in his book *Love Your God with All Your Mind*.

There have been people throughout history who have tried to squelch the healing ministry of Jesus. Some taught that the healing ministry stopped with the death of the last apostle, but early Christian writers in the third century, such as Justin Martyr, Irenaeus, and Origen, attest to almost the same range of healing happening in their time as those recorded in the gospel. The fact that divine healings are happening today shows that divine healing continues even in our time. Some dismiss the healing power of Jesus because they never saw it happen in their lives. They never took time to learn how to receive the divine power of Jesus and then use it to bring that power to people who desire it.

In the following pages, we will explore ways of tapping into the divine healing power and offering it to people in our care and in our lives. I have seen thousands of people improve and get well after receiving healing prayer. There is nothing more exciting than seeing a healing happen. I invite you to discover that excitement. You can be part of this divine healing ministry and carry Jesus' healing love every day. Jesus commissioned his followers to continue his healing ministry. You will be joining an awesome team of Christians who have been ministering divine healing power throughout the centuries.

We have to accept that there is a certain mystery about healing. We do not understand all the intricacies and why some people are healed and some are not as we wish. Even though we do not understand the mystery, we are still commissioned to do the ministry. In the Appendix of this book, we will see some things that can block healing from occurring and certain things that seem to make it happen more frequently.

As we delve into the gospels, one thing we do discover is that divine love is what heals. Jesus carried that divine love within himself, which set the environment for healing. The first disciples received the anointing of divine healing love at Pentecost when the Holy Spirit came upon them. This holy love allowed them to bring healing to the people they met. In my book *Healing Miracles in Act*

INTRODUCTION

of the Apostles, I describe eighteen healing miracles that happened through these early Christians. They needed to be baptized in the Holy Spirit and receive the gifts of the Holy Spirit to do the ministry of Jesus described in the gospels. As long as the early church baptized adults with the baptism of the Holy Spirit, the healings continued.

Knowing this, if you wish to be part of Jesus' healing ministry today, I recommend that you make a spiritual retreat to receive the full power and gifts of the Holy Spirit for your healing ministry. After I went through the Spiritual Enrichment Retreat, I felt the anointing and direction to do the healing ministry. When I was a student in Innsbruck, Austria, studying for the ministry, a priest led us through that Spiritual Enrichment Retreat. I made a full adult commitment, asking Jesus to be the Lord of my life, which opened me to the full power of the Holy Spirit. I felt Jesus' deep love for me like I had never experienced before. I had an intense desire to get to know him and listen to his direction for my life. It gave me a thirst to read the gospels and discover more about the ministry of Jesus. This baptism in the Holy Spirit empowered me to affect people's lives in a way that brought divine healing. We started praying with people for healing and we saw them get well. I became determined to discover the essential components that set the stage for a healing to occur.

For the next four years of graduate school, I studied every gospel healing story, read many books on Christian healing, and wrote my master's thesis on healing, which became my first book, *Arise and Walk*. That was forty-eight years ago, and through much more study and continual healing ministry, I discovered many facets of Jesus' healing ministry. I learned of ways every baptized Christian can participate in offering his healing love to those they meet. This book contains the fruits of my journey. That Spiritual Retreat can be found in my book, *Living a Transformed Life*. Videos are also available to help you journey through that spiritual time. All of these helped thousands of people get spiritually prepared for this divine healing ministry and gave them an accurate scriptural picture of God as revealed by Jesus. It also gave them a deep peace and serenity in their life.

Introduction

To uncover the treasures of the gospels regarding healing, we will look at twenty-nine healing accounts and explore what set the environment for these healings to happen. We will see Jesus' physical healings, emotional or inner healings, spiritual healings, and deliverances from evil. We will examine who played a part in the miracle and what we can learn about healing from each account to deepen our understanding and enrich our ability to offer healing. We will seek to experience what it was like to be there, to hear the discourse, to see the eyes, and to feel the wonder of the divine presence transforming someone's life.

If you have a group or community with whom you could make this journey, I suggest that as a helpful thing. There will be questions for discussion at the end of each healing story. There will also be some suggestions for ways to practice praying with someone for healing. Interspersed will be stories of healings that have happened in our day. There will also be references for deeper study. The experience gets richer the more we enter in and walk in the footprints of Jesus. We will go through the miracles somewhat in the order that they are accounted for in the gospels. There are obviously more miracles than those described in this book, but I believe these are the main ones from which we can draw insights into how and why Jesus did his ministry. They give us wisdom about how we can continue to offer his healing power in our world today.

THE HEALING ACCOUNTS

HEALING ACCOUNT 1

The Royal Official's Son

READ JOHN 4:46–54

46 Once more Jesus visited Cana in Galilee, where he had turned the water into wine. And there was a certain royal official whose son lay sick at Capernaum. 47 When this man heard that Jesus had arrived in Galilee from Judea, he went to him and begged him to come and heal his son, who was close to death.

48 "Unless you people see miraculous signs and wonders," Jesus told him, "you will never believe."

49 The royal official said, "Sir, come down before my child dies."

50 Jesus replied, "You may go. Your son will live."

The man took Jesus at his word and departed. 51 While he was still on the way, his servants met him with the news that his boy was living. 52 When he inquired as to the time when his son got better, they said to him, "The fever left him yesterday at the seventh hour."

53 Then the father realized that this was the exact time at which Jesus had said to him, "Your son will live." So he and all his household became believers.

REFLECTION

The royal official met Jesus and asked him to come and heal his son, who was sick. Jesus made a statement about faith. He said it must be deeper than just seeing miracles. The man recognized that Jesus was not refusing his request, so he asked again. Jesus offered him a promise that his son would live. The man trusted Jesus and started for home. On the way, he learned of his son's healing, which he recognized had occurred when Jesus said, "Your son will live." And then the powerful conclusion: "He and his whole household became believers."

The father displays some faith or trust that Jesus could heal his son, but by the end of the story, the father and his household enter into a faith relationship with Jesus. The first faith is just a belief that Jesus could do this, but the second faith is a life commitment to Jesus. This story, as well as other healing stories, tells us that the ultimate goal of the divine healing ministry is to demonstrate God's love for us and to draw us into a committed faith relationship with God. Spiritual healing is a significant goal of Jesus' healing ministry. He knew that if people did not make a faith commitment to him, they would not have the fullness of life that he desired for them. This goal was unique to Jesus' healing ministry and is an integral part of the Christian healing ministry today.

This new connection that this family had with Jesus is, I believe, what J. P. Moreland calls "attachment love." He describes this in his book *A Simple Guide to Experience Miracles*. He defines attachment love as "love that involves an intimate, close, experiential connection between those who love each other." He goes on to write, "We are created to function best in loving, relational dependence on God, and attaching to him in love is one of the central aims of Christianity." The healing ministry of Jesus invited people to that deep love connection. We will see in the healing accounts that once people experienced this attachment love by committing their life to him through faith, they were transformed. They were made whole. This attachment love is available to us through our faith commitment to Jesus.

The Royal Official's Son

The initial openness to Jesus' power to heal is essential to set an environment for his healing energy to flow. As healing ministers, we might try to establish an initial trust of faith by reading a healing story from scripture or telling a healing story to open a person's heart to receive healing. True worship music and worshipful singing of a community can also help set an environment for healing to happen. These things help us and the person to stay focused on Jesus, not the illness or wound.

In this account, Jesus' healing love was transferred from the father to the son without the son being present. We can pray for people at a distance and see healing results. God's love knows no bounds. I remember a time when we were celebrating a healing service in Malta. After sharing communion, we prayed for people, and many experienced healings. One of the priests present asked if we would pray for his sister. She could not be there that evening because she had fallen and hurt her leg. We did pray for her. The next day, when we were standing at the airport, ready to board our flight to the next country, this woman came running and jumping through the airport. She was the priest's sister. She told us that right at the time we prayed for her, her pain went away, and her leg was healed. She and her brother were very excited. The healing love of God had changed her even at a distance. As prayer ministers, it is important to be open to all the ways God desires to bring healing. We simply pray in his name and watch his love transform lives.

One thing we might notice about this gospel story is that the royal official worked for the occupying government that kept the people of Israel under control. Jesus could have been judgmental about this official, but instead, Jesus healed his son. Jesus' healing ministry challenges our healing ministry to be open to all people.

As we reflect on this account, we notice that three times John uses the word "life" or "live" as in, "your son is going to "live." The word used here for "life" is *Zoe* in Greek. It does not just mean physical life but a life connected to Jesus, the fullness of life. Jesus cured the boy to demonstrate his love, but more importantly, he did it so the whole family had a chance to "Live." They responded to Jesus' invitation by becoming believers. Now they would "live" because they were in a faith relationship with him. The uniqueness of Jesus' healing ministry is not that he cured people but that he cured them so that they had an opportunity to have "life" in its fullness, to be attached to him in love forever. Jesus said, "I have come that they might have life and have it to the full" (John 10:10).

We might consider how the royal official felt as he approached Jesus. He was part of the occupying government that controlled the Jews. How would he feel asking a healing favor from this Jewish Rabbi? Jesus' acceptance of him and his words, "You son will live," must have broken down many walls. How do you think his feelings changed after this encounter? As we minister Jesus' healing love, we can be aware that our gestures of love in Jesus' name can heal more than we can see with our eyes. Breaking down barriers between people and dispelling false judgments are important effects of the healing ministry.

Jesus introduced God as *Abba*, the Aramaic word for "daddy." He described God's deep love for us and that God wants us to be well and connect to him as closely as Jesus is connected to him (John 15:9). When we pray with people for healing, it is critical that we focus on *Abba's* love and desire to heal his children. We also can make them aware that the Holy Love of God, the Holy Spirit, is swirling around them, bringing physical, emotional, and spiritual healing. Any time we bring that awareness of God's love to a person, and they experience divine love, healing happens on some level. Our main role as healing ministers is to carry the deep love of God to the person who needs healing. Preparation for healing ministry begins with receiving God's extravagant love in prayer and quiet listening so we can offer this precious gift to people we meet.

THE ROYAL OFFICIAL'S SON

QUESTIONS TO PONDER/DISCUSS

- What did Jesus do or say that created an environment for healing?
- Why do you think this man trusted Jesus?
- What were the results of this healing encounter?
- What are the takeaways from this healing account?

HEALING ACCOUNT 2

The Man with an Evil Spirit

READ MARK 1:21-28 (THIS ACCOUNT IS ALSO RECORDED IN LUKE 4:31-37)

21 They went to Capernaum, and when the Sabbath came, Jesus went into the synagogue and began to teach. 22 The people were amazed at his teaching, because he taught them as one who had authority, not as the teachers of the law. 23 Just then a man in their synagogue who was possessed by an evil spirit cried out, 24 "What do you want with us, Jesus of Nazareth? Have you come to destroy us? I know who you are—the Holy One of God!"

25 "Be quiet!" said Jesus sternly. "Come out of him!" 26 The evil spirit shook the man violently and came out of him with a shriek.

27 The people were all so amazed that they asked each other, "What is this? A new teaching—and with authority! He even gives orders to evil spirits and they obey him." 28 News about him spread quickly over the whole region of Galilee.

REFLECTION

This account tells us about one of the times when Jesus demonstrated his power to dispel evil from a person. Jesus clearly has authority over evil. We notice here that evil manifests itself in the presence of

The Man with an Evil Spirit

Jesus. It is agitated by the divine presence. Jesus uses a simple word of command to send the evil out of the person. The response of the crowd indicates that this was a very unique occurrence.

Dispelling evil might be considered another level of the healing ministry. In training prayer ministers, I start with praying for healing, and after some experience, we talk about dealing with evil. The text mentions twice Jesus' authority. He is connected to the Author of life, so he can both teach and dispel evil through the power of that connection. We also have the authority to dispel evil by being connected to the Author. Jesus gave that authority to his disciples (Mark 6:7–12), and he gives it to us by receiving his Spirit at baptism. If we are going to minister to someone who may be oppressed by an evil spirit, we need to be very closely connected to Jesus. We need to be spiritually honest and sound. It is also good to have a team of people if possible.

We have often seen that if an evil spirit oppresses a person it clings to some wounded memory or area that needs inner healing. Sometimes evil comes out when we pray for healing of that inner wound. If evil clings to a wound, and we begin praising Jesus in a healing service, the evil may manifest itself and want to get out. At one of our healing services, during a healing prayer, a woman began feeling pain in her chest and then up her throat, and then there was like a release. She felt the pain for about fifteen minutes, and then it was gone. After that, she felt much better and had greater inner peace. I found out that she had some inner painful childhood memories, which is probably where the evil found residence. As she experienced the presence of Jesus during the worship and healing prayer, the evil wanted to flee. It manifested itself and then was gone. We then prayed inner healing prayers for the wounded memories where it had been clinging so it no longer had a place to reside in her.

The good, calming news is that evil cannot make us do anything unless we give it permission. It cannot possess us as Christians if we are filled with the presence of Jesus and his Holy Spirit. It can oppress us in areas of our wounds. It may oppress us even more if we have chosen it by being part of an occult, or we live with a repeated sin, or live with unforgiveness. There could also be an evil force lingering from our generational lines. In all these cases, we have the authority to dispel it through our connection to the Author of life. We need not fear. Often, we will gather a team of Christians who will stand with us to take authority and command the evil spirit to leave in Jesus' name.

Sometime, people come to me thinking they have an evil spirit in them. Repressed feelings, when they start coming up through some trigger, can feel like an outside force coming at them. I pray for inner healing first, and then, if there still seems to be something more than feelings, I pray a binding prayer to bind the power of evil and I command it to leave in Jesus' name. We each have the authority God gives us at our baptism to do this. Evil can be deceptive so if you are going to do deliverance prayer, further training on this subject is a good thing. For a deeper understanding of this ministry, you can contact Christian Healing Ministries at Christianhealingmin.org since they offer excellent training in this area of ministry. You may also want to read Francis and Judith MacNutt's book *Deliverance from Evil Spirits*.

Jesus came not only to forgive and heal but also to deliver people from the power of evil. He helps us take back what the devil has taken from us since the fall in the Garden of Eden. Evil has disrupted creation and caused tragedies throughout the centuries. It continues to do so. We can use our authority to bring peace and serenity where the forces of evil dwell.

In this passage, we read, "The people asked, 'What is this? A new teaching with authority.'" This demonstration of Jesus' power over evil is only a "teaching" because his disciples were watching. It speaks to us about the importance of mentoring others as we do his work. Having people join us when we pray with others is a natural way of mentoring more prayer ministers. We follow Jesus' example and use our authority based on the depth of our connection to the Author. Fostering a continual, deep relationship with Jesus is the source of power for all healing and deliverance ministry. We are called to use our God-given authority to free others of sickness and evil, and teach others to do the same.

THE MAN WITH AN EVIL SPIRIT

QUESTIONS TO PONDER/DISCUSS

- What was Jesus doing before his encounter with the man? What made him stop?
- What method of healing did Jesus use to bring wholeness to this man?
- Imagine being there in the synagogue. What do you think you would have felt?
- What wisdom can we glean from this account?

HEALING ACCOUNT 3

Simon's Mother-In-Law

READ MARK 1:29–31 (THIS ACCOUNT IS ALSO RECORDED IN MATTHEW 8:14–15 AND LUKE 4:38–39)

29 As soon as they left the synagogue, they went with James and John to the house of Simon and Andrew. 30 Simon's mother-in-law was in bed with a fever, and they told Jesus about her. 31 So he went to her, took her hand and helped her up. The fever left her and she began to wait on them.

REFLECTION

Imagine walking into Simon and Andrew's house after a morning of synagogue worship and smelling fresh baked bread and the aroma of garlic and onions sautéing in the pan. We can be there to experience the atmosphere as the women are preparing for a meal and the disciples start telling the story of how they just witnessed a demon being cast out by the power of Jesus' command. As they wait for the meal, they tell Jesus that Simon's mother-in-law is ill and Jesus responds immediately to bring healing.

The account tells us that Jesus took Simon's mother-in-law by the hand and helped her up. Jesus had just cast out an evil spirit in the synagogue with a powerful word of command, but here he used a tender, gentle gesture to bring his healing love. Each healing story is different because each situation is different. However, what is common to every story is that Jesus brought his divine love to every encounter and manifested it as needed for that situation. He conveyed the divine healing love in whatever way the person could best receive it. As ministers of healing, we must do the same. Sometimes, it is looking a person right in the eyes with divine love in our heart. Sometimes, it is laying our hands gently on them. (It is appropriate to ask for permission to touch someone if permission has not been implicitly given.) Sometimes we might convey Jesus' love through a phone call. The main thing is that we are overflowing with divine love and want to share it with the person to whom we are ministering.

Some people read this account and wonder where faith for healing was mentioned. As we journey through the healing accounts, we will notice that what creates the healing environment is Jesus' deep love connection with *Abba*. Jesus brings his deep "faith relationship" with *Abba* to every encounter. We go on to read that many people from that town came to Jesus to be in his presence, and in his presence, they experienced healing and deliverance. Then we discover the source of his power. We read that very early in the morning, he went off to a solitary place where he was "absorbed in prayer" (Mark 1:35). What he brought to Simon's mother-in-law and the people of that town was very special. It was divine, supernatural love. The good news is that we can do the same. We begin by being absorbed in prayer and then go out and share the gift. It takes some discipline to take quiet prayer time with God often, but it has awesome rewards.

As we examine more of the healing accounts, we will recognize that Jesus had a heart of compassion and wanted to help people get well. Jesus went right to Simon's mother-in-law and offered his healing love. As prayer ministers, we are called to develop a heart of compassion through our own inner work and prayer time. Then, we will become more attentive to people's needs and respond with healing love.

When someone comes to us in need, we listen, love, and pray. We listen to the person and the situation and then demonstrate Jesus' love in the way in which it can be best received. We pray that Jesus' love would flow over and through the person to bring healing. Jesus' presence, his Love, is the power that changes lives.

The account ends with Simon's mother-in-law waiting on Jesus and the disciples. Her healing is complete in the service of others. It is reminiscent of Jesus washing the feet of the disciples and then telling them they must do the same. No task is too small or insignificant when done in honor of God. Any service, any work, any ministry is holy when it is done for our Creator.

QUESTIONS TO PONDER/DISCUSS

- Jesus starts his ministry with a small group from his network of relationships (James and John, Simon and Andrew). Who might you invite to share in the healing ministry?
- What would have surprised you if you were a friend of Simon's mother-in-law in that house?
- Why did Jesus heal the way he did in this situation?
- What can we take away from this healing account?

PRACTICAL APPLICATION

If you aspire to being a prayer minister I suggest that you begin practicing praying with people in your group. One simple way is to stand in a circle, join hands, and pray quietly for the person to your left asking God's love to envelop them and heal any pains or illness that they may have. After a couple moments, you can pray for the person to your right. After you finish you may share what you felt during this prayer time.

HEALING ACCOUNT 4

The Man with Leprosy

READ MARK 1:40-45 (THIS ACCOUNT IS ALSO FOUND IN MATTHEW 8:1-4 AND LUKE 5:12-16)

40 A man with leprosy came to Jesus and begged him on his knees, "If you are willing, you can make me clean."
41 Filled with compassion, Jesus reached out his hand and touched the man. "I am willing," he said. "Be clean!"
42 Immediately the leprosy left him and he was cured.
43 Jesus sent him away at once with a strong warning:
44 "See that you don't tell this to anyone. But go, show yourself to the priest and offer the sacrifices that Moses commanded for your cleansing, as a testimony to them."
45 Instead he went out and began to talk freely, spreading the news. As a result, Jesus could no longer enter a town openly but stayed outside in lonely places. Yet people still came to him from everywhere.

REFLECTION

This healing happened early in Jesus' ministry and captures not only his compassionate heart but his willingness to risk his reputation to bring about healing. It was unlawful at that time to touch a leper, but Jesus was directed by a greater law, the divine law of caring for people. Jesus' message of loving your neighbor sometimes meant going past the human laws for the greater good. Doing the healing ministry today sometimes has these same risks regarding one's reputation, but as followers of Jesus, we do it anyway. Jesus' example here gives us the courage to do whatever it takes to minister divine healing love to those in need. This is especially true when we reach out to outcasts in our society. What other people think becomes secondary to what Jesus wants us to do.

The account says Jesus was "moved with compassion." It describes the main element of Jesus' healing ministry. This phrase in the New Testament is reserved to describe the heart of God. Many people apparently were unwilling to let their hearts be moved with compassion for this leper. We must be willing, as Jesus was, to let our hearts be moved by those who need healing and cleansing. We need to see beyond the exterior facade of people and see the need and inner person longing to be loved. In our quiet prayer time, we must be filled to overflowing with Jesus' love for us so that we develop a heart of compassion. Then we will respond to people as he did.

I recall one time early in my ordained ministry when we received a call that one of our community people had attempted suicide and was in the hospital. I went to the hospital to visit this woman and see what the issue was. As I walked in the door of her room, she screamed at me to get out. I quietly said, "I came because I care for you, and I want you to know that God loves you." I left because of her request, but the next day, I went back. This time, when I walked in, she still resisted my visit. I told her that God loved her and that I was going to be there if she wished to talk. At the next visit, she began to talk about her inner pain. This led to several months of conversations and inner healing prayer. All the inner pains eventually were released. The compassion of Jesus carried me through those first challenging visits which eventually led to this woman being healed.

The leper asked Jesus if he was willing to cleanse him. We must decide if we are willing to put in the effort and sometimes accept the risks of offering healing prayer to people we meet. Some will repel our offer, but we listen to Jesus' call and follow his direction. We listen to the person for the pain underneath the verbal response. At times, we may not be the person to minister to someone, but if we have a team, we may be able to discern who the right instrument is to bring healing in a particular situation.

Touch is a powerful way of transmitting the love of God. Jesus perceived that it was necessary in this case. He saw it as so essential that he did it at the risk of being considered unclean. As a prayer minister we may have to do similar things at times. We do whatever it takes to convey the healing love of God.

We might wonder why Jesus asked the man to show himself to the priest. The priest had to clear the man so he could return to town and be with people. It was part of the healing process since leprosy was not only a medical condition but also a social condition. This man had been an outcast for some time and needed to be integrated back into society by the priest. Part of our ministry may involve connecting people to healthy people in our community. Sometimes, it takes a healing community to soak a person in love and bring them to wholeness. If we can gather such a community, that is a treasure.

We might wonder why Jesus asked the man not to tell anyone about this healing. Part of the reason may be that then Jesus could not go into town because he had touched a leper. The people would have considered him unclean. But we see that the people in need "still came to him from everywhere" because their need was greater than the fear of letting Jesus touch them.

The other reason Jesus asked the man not to tell anyone is that the man had only experienced the physical cure. His skin was cleansed but Jesus came into the world to bring much more than just cures. The man did not yet understand that the greater healing was for him to enter into a faith relationship with Jesus, to commit his life to the life-giver. If he talked to people before he had this complete understanding, he would be proclaiming an incomplete message about Jesus. Jesus came to give the fullness of life through a relationship with him. When people entered into a faith relationship with him, he sent them to share his message of life and salvation. This man was not yet ready for that mission. We will see through the healing accounts that some people did commit to Jesus and some did not.

QUESTIONS TO PONDER/DISCUSS

- What was the cultural situation in this story?
- What part of the cultural laws does Jesus overlook?
- Why did Jesus minister healing the way he did?
- What can we learn from this healing account?

PRACTICAL APPLICATION

Stand in a circle, join hands, and try praying out loud for the person to your right, asking God's love to flow over them and through them to bring healing. After a few moments, do the same for the person on your left. After these prayers, invite people to share what they felt as you prayed. It takes practice and courage to pray out loud for someone but doing it together with people who are open to prayer is a good way to get comfortable with it.

HEALING ACCOUNT 5

The Paralytic

READ MARK 2:1-12

1 A few days later, when Jesus again entered Capernaum, the people heard that he had come home. 2 So many gathered that there was no room left, not even outside the door, and he preached the word to them. 3 Some men came bringing to him a paralytic, carried by four of them. 4 Since they could not get him to Jesus because of the crowd, they made an opening in the roof above Jesus and, after digging through it, lowered the mat the paralyzed man was lying on. 5 When Jesus saw their faith, he said to the paralytic, "Son, your sins are forgiven."

6 Now some teachers of the law were sitting there, thinking to themselves. 7 "Why does this fellow talk like that? He's blaspheming! Who can forgive sins but God alone?"

8 Immediately Jesus knew in his spirit that this was what they were thinking in their hearts, and he said to them, "Why are you thinking these things? 9 Which is easier to say to the paralytic, 'your sins are forgiven,' or to say, 'Get up, take your mat and walk'? 10 But that you may know that the Son of Man has authority on earth to forgive sins. . ." He said to the paralytic, 11 "I tell you, get up, take your mat and go home." 12 He got up, took his mat and walked out in full view of them all. This amazed everyone and they praised God, saying, "We have never seen anything like this!"

RELECTION

In this account, Jesus is "preaching the word" to the people, which sets the stage for a miracle. When we preach God's word today with power and passion and filled with his Spirit, we set the atmosphere for healing. People in the healing ministry have often reported that when someone preaches God's word, anointed by the Holy Spirit, miracles begin to happen as they follow it with prayer for healing. Randy Clark, a world-traveled healing minister, wrote, "Where there is the preaching to people who have not heard the gospel, the power to heal is present in an even greater degree, especially if the minister is open to the outpouring of the Holy Spirit." When preachers only talk about what is happening in the world or do not believe the stories in the gospel, they deprive people of the power that would be available to them. Speaking God's word with conviction is an important piece of the healing ministry. If we go to pray with someone, sharing a healing story from the scripture and talking about the healing power of God's love creates an openness to receiving God's healing.

We read in this account how Jesus is able to hear the deeper need of the man, and he responds to that need. We have learned that unrepented sin and unforgiveness can block divine healing power. It paralyzes us and keeps us from connecting to the Healer. Jesus could see this man would not walk unless he was freed from his sins. He responded to the core need so that the man's presenting need could be met. Once forgiven, the man was able to be healed and walk. When someone asks for healing prayer, it is important to discern if there is an issue beneath the need they are presenting. If prayer for forgiveness is needed, we begin with that. Listening to Jesus' messages and learning what things often lay beneath the surface of an illness or pain can help us pray for others.

Unforgiveness is one of the biggest blocks to healing. It can cause serious pain in our bodies. A woman came to me asking for prayer for her back pain. I asked, "When did it start? And what is going on in your life?" She mentioned a difficult situation that had made her very angry. I asked if she would be willing to forgive the

The Paralytic

person who caused the hurt and then release the hurt into Jesus' hands. This woman did forgive the offender and prayed a blessing prayer for him. Then the back pain went away.

Craig Miller has a very insightful book titled *Breaking Emotional Barriers to Healing*. He records many such healings and describes the underlying emotions for many physical illnesses and conditions. This scripture story challenges us to look deeper when an illness or pain occurs. Knowing this, plus bringing the healing love of Jesus to a person, can improve our way of helping people get well. It gives hope to many who have prayed for something without any visible results. We do not always see total cures, but if a person feels Jesus's deep love for them and his readiness to forgive, some healing will always happen. We might be one person on the list of people that Jesus is calling to pray with them. Doing our part sets the stage for the next level of healing.

When we pray for someone, it is crucial to listen for God's directions so that the healing is thorough and complete. What people express to us may be only the tip of a deeper affliction or inner wound. Sometimes, when I have prayed with a person, one of the people on our team would hear a word from God. A team member once said, "I have a picture of a waterfall. Does this mean anything to you?" That picture took the person back to the original situation where their pain began. It opened them to releasing the pain and feeling relief. This is called a "word of knowledge." It is a gift of the Holy Spirit that can help bring healing to someone in need. God's word opens the way for release and healing.

In this account, the man's friends make sacrifices to get him in the presence of Jesus. Our role as Christians is to get people into the presence of Jesus so that they can experience forgiveness and healing. We sometimes have to push through the initial barriers. Imagine being these men and climbing on the roof, digging the hole, taking the risk, but then watching their friend get off his mat. The effort and the risk were well worth it. Our faith in Jesus gives us the courage to move through the resistance and carry out our ministry. These men had to get up on the roof and dig a hole so that they could get their friend in Jesus' presence. It is important to recognize that we do not heal people. We get them in a place where they can experience Jesus' healing presence. We do what it takes to create an environment for them to receive what Jesus wants to do in their lives. We use whatever gifts God has given us to offer divine healing power.

The paralyzed man had great trust in his friends. If we aspire to be a prayer minister, we must be trustworthy. We build trust by our life witness and by listening to the person and showing compassion for their need. We don't say what we don't know; we do say what we do know. We know that Jesus wants people to be well and connected to him. We build trust by staying in Jesus' word and only doing what he did with gentleness and humility.

It is interesting to see the people's response to this miracle. Some respond with indignation because Jesus told the man his sins were forgiven. Others responded with amazement, and they began to praise God. Responses to Jesus' healing ministry happening today are similar. Some people try to squelch it, and others are amazed and seek ways to carry it out. You can expect those responses if you desire to participate in this ministry. It is God's call for every Christian to offer his healing love, and I encourage you to pray with people to the extent that you can. A person's response to your efforts is their business.

When someone is healed or relieved from pain, it is important to share the story, for it encourages people to participate in Jesus' healing and saving mission. It is also important to praise God as the people did in the story. It keeps the focus on God and not on us. We are only "earthen vessels" carrying a precious ointment to people in need.

One last note: When the "teachers of the law" said that only God can forgive sins, they were thinking accurately. What they struggled to believe is that Jesus was God. The healing validated his ability to forgive sins, proving that he was God. This story was used in the history of the church to prove that Jesus was Divine. He shared his divine power with us by sending the Holy Spirit so that we could continue his ministry.

The Paralytic

QUESTIONS TO PONDER/DISCUSS

- What was the setting for this miracle? What would it have felt like to be there?
- Why did Jesus do this miracle the way he did?
- How do we bring people into the presence of Jesus?
- What can we take away from this account?

PRACTICAL APPLICATION

Break into groups of two. One person can ask for prayer for some physical, emotional, or spiritual healing. Then, the other person prays, either out loud or quietly, a simple prayer for healing. Then switch roles and do the same.

HEALING ACCOUNT 6

The Woman at the Well

READ JOHN 4:4-17, 28-32, 39-42

4 Now Jesus had to go through Samaria. 5 So he came to a town in Samaria called Sychar, near the plot of ground Jacob had given to his son Joseph. 6 Jacob's well was there, and Jesus, tired as he was from the journey, sat down by the well. It was about the sixth hour.

7 When a Samaritan woman came to draw water, Jesus said to her, "Will you give me a drink?" 8 (His disciples had gone into the town to buy food.)

9 The Samaritan woman said to him. "You are a Jew and I am a Samaritan woman. How can you ask me for a drink?" (For Jews do not associate with Samaritans.)

10 Jesus answered her, "If you knew the gift of God and who it is that asks you for a drink, you would have asked him and he would have given you living water."

11 "Sir," the woman said, "you have nothing to draw water with and the well is deep. Where do you get this living water? 12 Are you greater than our father Jacob, who gave us the well and drank from it himself, as did also his sons and his flocks and herds?"

13 Jesus answered, "Everyone who drinks this water will be thirsty again, 14 but whoever drinks the water I give will never thirst. Indeed, the water I give him will become in him a spring of water welling up to eternal life."

The Woman at the Well

15 The woman said to him, "Sir, give me this water so that I won't be thirsty and have to keep coming here to draw water."
16 He told her, "Go, call your husband and come back."
17 "I have no husband," she replied. Jesus said to her, "You are right when you say you have no husbands. 18 The fact is, you have had five husbands and the man you now have is not your husband. What you have just said is quite true.".. .
28 Then, leaving her water jar, the woman went back to the town and said to the people. 29 "Come, see a man who told me everything I ever did. Could this be the Christ?" 30 They came out of the town and made their way toward him.
31 Meanwhile his disciples urged him, "Rabbi, eat something."
32 But he said to them, "I have food to eat that you know nothing about." . . .
39 Many of the Samaritans from that town believed in him because of the woman's testimony, "He told me everything I ever did." 40 So when the Samaritans came to him, they urged him to stay with them, and he stayed two days. 41 And because of his words many more became believers.
42 They said to the woman, "We no longer believe just because of what you said; now we have heard for ourselves, and we know that this man really is the Savior of the world."

REFLECTION

This is not an account of physical healing, but it is an important story about inner healing. It informs us about another facet of Jesus' healing ministry. He not only cured people of their physical pain but offered inner healing of their wounded hearts and memories that weighed them down. His healing ministry was holistic. He did not only care for their body, but he was attentive to people's emotional needs and their spiritual wellness. He wanted people to be well forever. We can draw much hope from looking closely at how he ministered to people and learning how he wants to minister to us.

This story shows Jesus' desire to get to the core issue of human woundedness. He is aware of the dynamics of our being, and he desires that we live the fullness of life. We are meant to live each day in his presence filled with his joy and peace. He is concerned with healing our physical conditions and healing our hearts and our souls.

This story of Jesus' encounter with the woman at the well demonstrates the power of his love to bring about a deep, inner healing. The woman was not at the well in the morning with the other women of the village, but she came out on her own at noon. Perhaps she was ashamed or shunned for her life with many men. Jesus' inviting question, his promise of life-giving water, and his pure, divine love allowed this woman to experience a love relationship that filled her deepest longing for true love. Jesus' gentle way broke down the barriers that kept her in the prison of her pain. She had been looking for love with various men, but her wounded heart tempted her to attach herself to destructive relationships. These relationships were holding her back from discovering real life. Jesus' love gave her a chance to experience what real love is like, and it offered her an opportunity to heal her deep inner wounds.

Jesus offers a model for inner healing prayer. His acceptance of this woman, even though she was a Samaritan, breaks through the walls that existed between Jews and Samaritans. His request helps her break through her personal defenses and begins a healing conversation. His promise of a life filled with living water, which symbolizes his unconditional love, created an openness in her to listen and to begin trusting his words. Though challenging, his request to call her husband allowed her to get free of the way that she had been relating to men. Each statement paved the way for healing this woman's self-esteem and inner pains.

The sign of her healing becomes evident as she puts down her water jar and goes back into town. She was now the vessel filled with life-giving water. This encounter changed her and freed her to go back to the people she had been avoiding earlier that day and courageously invite them to meet Jesus. She goes back and invites them to come and meet the Life-giver. The fact that they follow her out to the well is a testimony that she changed significantly and that inner healing had occurred. It must have been clear that she had not just met the seventh man. The people of the town could see that she was a different woman. Her eyes, her voice, her demeanor must have spoken of a huge transformation. Why else would they follow her out to meet Jesus?

After the people of the town met Jesus, they invited him to stay in their town. He stayed two days. Many of those people needed inner healing as well. Most people need some level of inner healing to work through emotional pains or release traumatic memories. Jesus wants us to be free of the parts of our story that weigh on us and wear down our physical health.

These inner repressed emotions have a negative effect on our physical body. The Centers for Disease Control and Prevention states that 92 percent of physical illnesses have an emotional root. In his book, *Breaking Emotional Barriers to Healing*, Craig Miller offers the following statistics. He writes, "Research details the influence of stress and the importance of expressing emotions to assist in healing and healthy living. Up to 98 percent of mental, physical, and behavioral illness comes from our thought life. Stress is a factor in 75 percent of all illnesses and diseases. Eighty-eight percent of cancers are due to lifestyle and not genetics. Seventy-five to ninety percent of all visits to the primary care doctor are due to stress-related problems."

These numbers may indicate why Jesus offered inner healing to this woman and why it is so important for us to receive inner healing and help people deal with their inner pains. Even in the stories of physical healing, Jesus' accepting love and affirmation also brought inner healing. His efforts to change people's thinking from just a human worldview to a divine worldview of themselves were also part of the emotional and spiritual healing of his ministry. This change in people's way of thinking releases stress. These things broaden the picture of Jesus' healing ministry beyond the physical change. His heart hurt when people were in pain, and he desired to make them whole, to have the fullness of life. The uniqueness of Jesus' healing ministry is that it was holistic. He wanted people to be healthy in mind, body, and soul and to be with him forever.

We do notice in the healing accounts that Jesus could physically cure a person because of his intense love for them. He loved with the same love that brought them into existence. If they wished to be emotionally healed, they had to make some decisions. The woman had to go and call her husband. Others had to repent or forgive. They had to participate in their journey to wellness. If people wanted to be spiritually healthy, they had to make a faith commitment to Jesus. They had to enter into a relationship with him. This woman made a faith commitment to Jesus, and his healing love empowered her to invite others into a faith commitment. The end of the story tells us that many more became believers in Jesus. He could not force these faith commitments but only invite people to the fullness of life. The same is true today. I have seen people get physically cured. Some followed Jesus from that time on, and some walked away and continued their lifestyle. Our mission is to invite them into wholeness so they have an opportunity to be well forever.

Most of my ministry through the years has been in the area of inner healing. Often, when we were able to go back to the core issue, the first experience of pain, and invite a person to feel Jesus' presence in that place, they experienced the release of pain and healing. In many cases, this brought about greater physical health. The basic pattern is that the prayer minister invites Jesus to take the person back in their memory to the core issue and let his love release and heal repressed emotions and wounded memories. Many physical healings happen after such an inner journey.

I must mention that if you feel called to minister inner healing, it is important to get good training. Christian Healing Ministries in Jacksonville Florida (Christianhealingmin.org), OSL South Carolina (oslcharleston.com), and the Order of St. Luke (osltoday.org) offer good training for this ministry. There are many great books on inner healing, some of which are found in the "Books for Further Reading" section at the back of this book. Inner healing ministry is more difficult than praying with someone for physical healing. It involves listening skills and knowing what to do when painful memories surface. With study and practice, you can learn these skills and develop the underlying spiritual foundation to carry out this ministry. Having a professional counselor on your team is also good for dealing with hidden issues that may be beyond your giftedness.

This scripture account makes us aware of the need to be attentive to the inner pains that people carry. We notice in the story how Jesus gently persisted in inviting this woman to go past her defenses and let go of her inner pain. He could see her inner hurt and could not walk away without giving her a chance to be made well. In the story, the woman models the power of Jesus' love to heal the child within us and free our memories of the wounds we carry. Her return to the village, filled with this new anointing, emboldens us to invite people into the inner healing power of Jesus' pure love. Every time we listen to Jesus' voice and allow his presence to heal and to fill our "vessel," we are being readied to pour his love on others. Listening, loving, and praying in Jesus' name are the main ingredients in helping people on the road to wellness.

Jesus' ministry not only changed people's physical condition but also offered healing to the whole person. His ministry was much more holistic than the other healers of his day. He knew that people's inner pains were destructive to their physical wellness. He knew that medicine stopped short of getting at the core issues and bringing about lasting health. His healing ministry was unique to the world, and we are privileged to share in it. We can experience the type of healing that he offers and we can offer this precious gift to others.

QUESTIONS TO PONDER/DISCUSS

- What elements do you see in the story that are part of an inner healing encounter?
- Have you ever experienced inner healing prayer? What did it feel like?
- Is this a ministry that you would like to explore?
- What can we learn from this healing account?

PRACTICAL APPLICATION

Ask God to show you any areas in your life that need inner healing. Imagine being with this woman at the well and listening to Jesus' words and feeling his love. Let his love soak through you and release any heaviness that you carry inside. Begin thanking Jesus for being there with you desiring to set you free. Like the woman, share this story with someone who may also need inner healing.

HEALING ACCOUNT 7

The Man at the Pool Side

READ JOHN 5:1-17

1 Some time later, Jesus went up to Jerusalem for a feast of the Jews. 2 Now there is in Jerusalem near the Sheep Gate a pool, which in Aramaic is called Bethesda and which is surrounded by five covered colonnades. 3 Here a great number of disabled people used to lie—the blind, the lame, the paralyzed. 5 One who was there had been an invalid for thirty-eight years. 6 When Jesus saw him lying there and learned that he had been in this condition for a long time, he asked him, "Do you want to get well?" 7 "Sir," the invalid responded, "I have no one to help me into the pool when the water is stirred. While I am trying to get in, someone else goes down ahead of me."
8 Then Jesus said to him, "Get up! Pick up your mat and walk." 9 At once the man was cured; he picked up his mat and walked.
The day on which this took place was a Sabbath, 10 and so the Jews said to the
man, who had been healed, "It is the Sabbath; the law forbids you to carry your mat."
11 But he replied, "The man who made me well said to me, 'pick up your mat and walk.'"
12 So they asked him, "Who is this fellow who told you to pick it up and walk?"

13 The man who was healed had no idea who it was, for Jesus had slipped way into the crowd that was there.
14 Later Jesus found him at the temple and said to him, "See, you are well again. Stop sinning or something worse may happen to you." 15 The man went away and told the Jews that it was Jesus who had made him well. 16 So, because Jesus was doing this on the Sabbath, the Jews persecuted him. 17 Jesus said to them, "My Father is always at his work to this day, and I, too, am working."

REFLECTION

Jesus' question, "Do you want to get well," is the central question of this account. The Greek word tells us that the man was "cured," but he was not made well. He could walk, but his heart and soul were still paralyzed. Jesus could cure the man who did not even know him because his love was that intense. However, Jesus could not make this man well because that involved his willingness to change his behavior and enter into a faith relationship with Jesus. Jesus found him in the temple later and invited him to change his ways if he wanted to be whole. The man remained a victim of his own choices, despite Jesus' invitation to make him well. He went off and reported Jesus to the Jewish leaders. He never received the "fullness of life" (John 10:10).

It is hard to tell why Jesus chose to cure this man and not any other. Perhaps because the man had been in that condition for so long, Jesus chose to reach out to him. Perhaps Jesus felt that once cured the man would follow him and become a disciple, but Jesus could not make that happen. The journey to wholeness and real life is each person's choice. As we do Jesus' healing ministry, we will see people get cured or get better, yet like Jesus, we will not be able to make them whole unless they choose to commit their lives to Jesus. We pray for cures and then invite people into the fullness of life found in a relationship with Jesus. We can give them the first part, but they must participate in receiving the second part. Only in a life with Jesus are we whole.

The Man at the Pool Side

This man acts like a victim. He blames others for his inability to get well, but as the story progresses, we discover that he needs to change his behavior to get well. Like the story we explored earlier, his sins had paralyzed him. We may run into people who play the victim role. They blame others for their situation, but they do not take responsibility for their actions. Jesus challenges him to change his behavior. Sometimes the healing ministry calls us to be radically honest with a person. They may get angry at us for such a challenge. If we have built up a trusting relationship, we may be able to approach some tough subjects with them. If they know we truly care and want the best for them, they may break out of their victim mentality and begin to get well. If we offer to support them on the journey to wellness, they may be willing to make the journey. I watched many people in our AA and Alanon groups make the journey to freedom. Inviting them to a love relationship with Jesus was often a huge part of that road to new life and wholeness.

As we seek to help people get well, we must listen closely to what they are saying. Sometimes, people are receiving a subconscious reward to remain in their situation. Maybe they get extra attention, care, sympathy, or entitlement and do not have to work. If this is the case, they will not want to get well. Offering them the love and security of Jesus and a gentle conversation can help them step beyond these smaller rewards to a greater fullness of life. Listening to Jesus as we minister may afford us the right words to walk with someone to the greater rewards of a healthy life.

We can only grow to the capacity of our worldview. This man goes off and reports Jesus to the authorities. He could not see Jesus as anything more than a person who was not following the Jewish law. He could not appreciate the gift of the cure he had just received. He did not take the opportunity to see the world as Jesus did. He ends up participating in getting Jesus killed in Jerusalem. As ministers of healing, we may not always receive a reward for our efforts, but Jesus knows that we are being faithful to him and his ministry. As we saw earlier, there can be a sacrifice in trying to bring someone to wholeness. The sacrifice diminishes knowing we are participating in Jesus' divine mission.

There is no mention of faith on the part of the paralyzed man. He did not even know who Jesus was. His cure is brought about by the intense divine love that Jesus brought to that poolside. Divine love is what cures people. Our role is to carry divine love to every encounter.

QUESTIONS TO PONDER/DISCUSS

- Why does Jesus ask the question, "Do you want to get well?"
- What are the significant elements of healing found in this story?
- Have you met people who do not want to get well?
- What can we learn about healing from this account?

PRACTICAL APPLICATION

If you have a group, have half the people sit in a row of chairs, and the other half of the group stand behind them. Those standing lay hands on the shoulders of those sitting and quietly soak them in God's love. Then, after a time, they change roles.

HEALING ACCOUNT 8

The Man with a Shriveled Hand

READ MARK 3:1-6 (THIS ACCOUNT IS ALSO FOUND IN MATTHEW 12:9-14 AND LUKE 6:6-11)

1 Another time Jesus went into the synagogue, and a man with a shriveled hand was there. 2 Some of them were looking for a reason to accuse Jesus, so they watched him closely to see if he would heal him on the Sabbath.

3 Jesus said to the man with the shriveled hand, "Stand up in front of everyone."

4 Then Jesus asked them, "Which is lawful on the Sabbath: to do good or to do evil, to save life or to kill?" But they remained silent.

5 He looked around at them in anger and, deeply distressed at their stubborn hearts, said to the man, "Stretch out your hand." He stretched it out, and his hand was completely restored.

6 Then the Pharisees went out and began to plot with the Herodians how they might kill Jesus.

REFLECTION

In this account, we read of Jesus going into the synagogue to take time for worship and perhaps to preach. We read that his life was filled with special moments to stay connected to *Abba*.

He sustained his ministry with that deep love connection. His example speaks to us of the value of such a relationship.

Jesus' healing ministry was central to his preaching and teaching. Even though he may have come to the synagogue for prayers or preaching, he is moved to offer a cure for this afflicted man. Even though he knew that the Jewish leaders were waiting for a chance to accumulate evidence against him, his heart of compassion moved him to offer this cure. Jesus gave life at the cost of his life. His amazing love was not to be stopped.

Jesus cured this man to proclaim that the Sabbath was a day to save life, set people free, pause from everyday things, and proclaim the incredible love of God. He did this at the risk of his own life. The leaders sought to kill him for this demonstration of his power on the Sabbath. Jesus accepted the risk because the gift was too important not to be given, and the message was too important not to be spoken. We may be ridiculed for offering healing prayer, but as disciples of Jesus, we must not stop. Too many people are in need; many will receive ministry only through us. Like Jesus, we accept the sacrifice of proclaiming his healing love. The God of the universe has chosen to work through us to continue this essential ministry. He relies on and resides within us to carry on this remarkable work.

Jesus uses an interesting and logical principle to confront the Jewish leaders watching him. He says, "Which is lawful on the Sabbath: to do good or to do evil, to save life or to kill?" Jesus is all about saving lives on any given day. The Jewish leaders had no answer, at least none they were willing to admit. People walking outside an abortion clinic asked the same question. Is it lawful to save a life or to kill it? Jesus is about saving lives today.

This account says that Jesus was angry at their stubborn hearts. It hurt his compassionate heart to see how these so-called religious leaders tried to stop him from doing good. We may feel a similar anger at people who do not want us to offer life and hope to people in need. They stand behind a law that stops the healing and saving ministry of Jesus. Jesus was not to be stopped. The old law of certain work on the Sabbath was less important than the saving and healing of a life. As ministers of healing, we have to make certain decisions. We do not harm but we also do not back away from doing good. There is a certain skepticism in our culture and even in our churches about the effectiveness of healing prayer. As Christians we are commissioned by Jesus to offer this gift to our world. We must not stop. We learn from the Master.

The Sabbath was supposed to be a day of freedom, an important day to celebrate life and give thanks for the life that God has given. In our culture, that purpose has somewhat been lost. It is important that we pause from regular work to give life to each other in worship. We are revitalized by worshipping God and celebrating with our community. This is the new Sabbath, the new day of hope, and the new day to honor our Creator.

Randy Clark, a world-known minister of healing, wrote in his book, *The Healing Breakthrough*, "There is such priceless value to having the God of the universe working in and through us." He wrote of the excitement of being in the presence of God as healing flowed through him. He also spoke of a time when the level of anointing and healing presence diminished in him. He prayed, asking God to show him if he had done anything wrong or grieved God in any way. He asked God not to leave him alone without his presence in him. Not long after that, he again could see the presence of God moving through him in healing. The Sabbath is a good time to revitalize ourselves in the presence of God through inner quieting, intentional listening, worship, and a renewed surrender to his will. We can pray each week for more anointing, more wisdom, and more peace.

The last sentence of this account indicates that Jesus passion began here. A group of religious leaders were planning his death for years. Their threats did not distract Jesus from his intense desire to bring healing and salvation to the world. Nothing would stop him from manifesting supernatural love in every situation. He would "do good" every day of the week. Ultimately, he would pay the price of his life to give life as he did. He continues to offer this healing love to us.

QUESTIONS TO PONDER/DISCUSS

- Where is faith, and where is love in this account?
- What was the context of this healing account? How does it speak about Jesus' healing ministry?
- Why did Jesus handle this situation the way he did?
- What can we learn from this account?

PRACTICAL APPLICATION

If you are alone or have a group, have each find some quiet spot and ask Jesus to anoint you with new power, presence, and wisdom to carry out his healing ministry. Take time to soak in his love.

HEALING ACCOUNT 9

The Centurion's Servant

READ MATTHEW 8:5-13 (THIS ACCOUNT IS ALSO FOUND IN LUKE 7:1-10)

5 When Jesus had entered Capernaum, a centurion came to him, asking for help. 6 "Lord," he said, "my servant lies at home paralyzed and in terrible suffering."

7 Jesus said to him, "I will go and heal him."

8 The centurion replied, "Lord, I do not deserve to have you come under my roof. But just say the word, and my servant will be healed. 9 For I myself am a man under authority, with soldiers under me. I tell this one, 'Go,' and he goes, and that one, 'Come,' and he comes. I say to my servant, 'Do this,' and he does it."

10 When Jesus heard this, he was astonished and said to those following him, "I tell you the truth, I have not found anyone in Israel with such great faith. 11 I say to you that many will come from the east and the west, and will take their places at the feast with Abraham, Isaac, and Jacob in the kingdom of heaven. But the subjects of the kingdom will be thrown outside, into the darkness, where there will be weeping and gnashing of teeth."

13 Then Jesus said to the centurion, "Go! It will be done just as you believed it would." And his servant was healed at that very hour.

REFLECTION

Jesus' immediate response to the request of this centurion is, "I will go and cure him." There is no better time to offer the healing love of Jesus than when the request is made. My mentor taught me that, if possible, it would be best to pray with a person right when they request it. It is the anointed moment. It seems Jesus was always ready to offer healing when he felt a need. His immediate response may be because the centurion said his servant was "in terrible suffering." Jesus hurt when people hurt, and he responded with healing relief. As followers of Jesus, he is our model.

Jesus' healing ministry shows that he sought to eliminate the suffering from illness, injury, sin, and the grip of evil, but he accepted the suffering and risk involved in carrying out his ministry. One form of suffering he healed, while the other he accepted and made holy for the benefit of his people. The energy and cost we expend to learn about and do the healing ministry of Jesus is made holy as we offer his healing love.

The power of divine healing is unlimited. It moves over distances to set people free. We read how distance is not a barrier to healing. We saw this in an earlier account. We can convey the healing love of Jesus to someone in need, which makes it possible to cross long distances. I have heard people say they could feel Jesus' healing love over the phone and through a zoom meeting. There are no limits.

The centurion felt unworthy to have Jesus in his house, but Jesus' words let him know that he was worthy. He was not a Jew, but Jesus demonstrated that his healing love was for all people. We may find people who feel unworthy of prayer for healing. They feel that they do not deserve it. They may have a great amount of shame inside from their family of origin, which makes them feel unworthy of such a gift. We must demonstrate by our actions that Jesus came to heal and save all people. Our presence, compassion, and care can dissolve the feelings of unworthiness and shame in others and allow them to feel the life-giving power of Jesus' love.

The Centurion's Servant

Our worthiness is not based on who we are but on who he is. He has made us worthy.

Typically, a Jew would not enter the house of a Gentile because he would incur ritual uncleanness. Maybe the centurion meant to spare Jesus this inconvenience when he said, "I do not deserve to have you come under my roof." Jesus, however, is ready to accept ritual uncleanness to offer healing to his servant who is in terrible suffering. His compassion was greater than his concern about ritual laws. We must step through barriers when we try to bring Jesus' healing to people. When our compassion grows, we become less concerned about what others think of us.

Sometimes, people may be suffering from what some call "cold love." They do not let Jesus love them totally as he wishes, and they do not receive love from people when it is offered to them. It is a challenge to get to the heart of these people. If we have a healing community, and we can get them to join in the life and activities of that community, then eventually, they may be warmed up and soak in some authentic love. They may need to meet the right person in the community who can break through the barrier and touch their longing heart. Jesus' healing happens in many different ways.

QUESTIONS TO PONDER/DISCUSS

- How does the cultural context make this story interesting?
- Have you ever experienced suffering for doing what Jesus asks of you?
- Are there times that you have felt unworthy of the love that God has for you?
- What messages can we glean from this healing account?

PRACTICAL APPLICATION

Prayer at a distance. Take a quiet moment and listen to Jesus. Which person in need do you sense he would like you to pray for? Which person comes to your mind or heart? Take some time and quietly pray for that person. You may wish to call them and pray. Later, you might check with them if they have felt anything.

HEALING ACCOUNT 10

The Widow's Son

READ LUKE 7:11-17

11 Soon afterward, Jesus went to a town called Nain, and his disciples and large crowd went along with him. 12 As he approached the town gate, a dead person was being carried out—the only son of his mother, and she was a widow. And a large crowd from the town was with her. 13 When the Lord saw her, his heart went out to her and he said, "Don't cry."

14 Then he went up and touched the coffin, and those carrying it stood still. He said, "Young man, I say to you, get up!" 15 The dead man sat up and began to talk, and Jesus gave him back to his mother.

16 They were all filled with awe and praised God. "A great prophet has appeared among us," they said. "God has come to help his people." 17 This news about Jesus spread throughout Judea and the surrounding country.

REFLECTION

Again, in this account, we see that Jesus' heart is moved with compassion for the person hurting the most: the mother of the boy. He could not pass by without a response of love and compassion. When someone has lost a loved one, our healing presence is a source of comfort for the person's family. Sometimes, the quiet, healing presence is the most effective in bringing comfort and peace to the family. I have often stood quietly by a widow or widower during a wake. There were no words to say. A quiet faith presence conveyed Jesus' healing and comforting love.

This account says that a large crowd was following Jesus, and a large crowd was following the mother of the boy. The two crowds met in the story, and the people in both groups needed to hear and see that Jesus had the power to raise the dead. Jesus said to the widow's dead son, "Young man, I say to you, arise." Jesus did not raise every person from the dead. Tradition tells us that Joseph, Jesus' earthly father, died before his public ministry. Jesus did not raise his own father from the dead, but he raised this boy to show his compassion and to demonstrate that he has the power to give life. The words, "arise" (*egertheti*) that Jesus says to the boy is the same word used to describe the resurrection of Jesus. This story hints at the gift of eternal life for all who hear Jesus' voice and respond to it. Jesus won this gift for us by his death and resurrection. The boy responds to the words of Jesus, and he receives the gift of new life. We will see in many healing stories that those who respond to Jesus' words receive healing and new life. As healing ministers, we seek to offer Jesus' words of life to those to whom we minister.

I have never seen someone raised from the dead, but I have heard of it happening. Dr. Chauncey Crandall, a well-known heart surgeon, in his book, *Raising the Dead: A Doctor Encounters the Miraculous*, tells the story of a man who was pronounced dead in the emergency room and then came back to life. I read a story about a group of young people on a mission in South America. They felt called to pray over a baby who had been dead for a couple days, and the baby came back to life. Knowing that these things happen widens our worldview and opens us to the awesome power of God in our world. If the dead can be raised, all is possible with God. In these cases, the praying person was listening to God's voice and heard a specific call to pray for the raising of the dead person. I have never heard that call, but I stay attentive to it. It is important that we listen to God's direction no matter to whom we are ministering.

This account reminds us that sickness and death affect a whole "crowd" of people—the family and friends. We are called to be attentive to the whole family as we offer Jesus' healing love. Inviting family members to pray with us for a loved one who is ill can be a source of healing for them. We may be part of helping a family work through unresolved issues. We can bring the healing presence of Jesus to all who are part of the "crowd."

Jesus seemed to be attentive to the people who were in the most desperate need. This widow not only lost her son, she lost her livelihood. She no longer had a means of income. We cannot help everyone, but we may be called to help specific people according to Jesus' direction. Listening to the voice of Jesus is an integral part of the spirituality of healing. When the voice of Jesus directs us, we see the divine power at work in us.

Jesus' ministry included teaching. In this story, Jesus sees a large crowd and teaches them by raising this boy from the dead. Praying for healing is a wonderful way of teaching people about the transforming power of God's love. We can bring the message of his compassion to many situations. The story tells us that the people in the crowds "were all filled with awe and praised God." Our ministry can direct people's attention to the many blessings that come from God. It leads to praise and worship of God.

We may have noticed that Jesus' first words to the boy's mother are, "Don't cry." When someone is grieving, we want to give them permission to cry and express their grief. Tears flush the toxins out of our system. Since Jesus knew what he would do, he did not minister to the widow's grief but invited her not to be afraid. His statement makes sense if we look at the outcome of this story. As healing minsters, we often must give people a safe place to express their grief by listening and offering comfort. When there are no words to say, comfort is given without words.

QUESTIONS TO PONDER/DISCUSS

- How does the context of the healing make it a teaching moment for both crowds?
- Why do you think Jesus ministered to this widow as opposed to others in a similar situation?
- Do you see any expression of faith in this story?
- What might we receive from this account?

PRACTICAL APPLICATION

Think of someone who is grieving. What is the source of their loss? Either pray quietly for them or contact them and see how Jesus directs you to minister to them.

HEALING ACCOUNT 11

The Gerasene Demoniac

READ MARK 5:1-20 (THIS ACCOUNT IS ALSO RECORDED IN MATTHEW 8:28-34 AND LUKE 8:26-39)

1 They went across the lake to the region of the Gerasenes. 2 When Jesus got out of the boat, a man with an evil spirit came from the tombs to meet him. 3 This man lived in the tombs, and no one could bind him anymore, not even with a chain. 4 For he had often been chained hand and foot, but he tore the chains apart and broke the irons on his feet. No one was strong enough to subdue him. 5 Night and day among the tombs and in the hills, he would cry out and cut himself with stones.

6 When he saw Jesus from a distance, he ran and fell on his knees in front of him. 7 He shouted at the top of his voice, "What do you want with me, Jesus, Son of the Most High God? Swear to God that you won't torture me!" 8 For Jesus had said to him, "Come out of this man, you evil spirit!"

9 Then Jesus asked him, "What is your name?" "My name is Legion," he replied, "for we are many." 10 And he begged Jesus again and again not to send them out of the area.

11 A large herd of pigs was feeding on the nearby hillside. 12 The demons begged Jesus, "Send us among the pigs; allow us to go into them." 13 He gave them

permission and the evil spirits came out and went into the pigs. The herd, about two thousand in number, rushed down the steep bank into the lake and were drowned.

14 Those tending the pigs ran off and reported this in the town and countryside, and the people went out to see what happened. 15 When they came to Jesus, they saw the man who had been possessed by the legion of demons, sitting there, dressed and in his right mind; and they were afraid. 16 Those who had seen it told the people what had happened to the demon-possessed man—and told about the pigs as well. 17 Then the people began to plead with Jesus to leave their region.

18 As Jesus was getting into the boat, the man who had been demon-possessed begged to go with him. 19 Jesus did not let him, but said, "Go home to your family and tell them how much the Lord has done for you, and how he has had mercy on you." 20 So the man went away and began to tell in the Decapolis how much Jesus had done for him. And all the people were amazed.

REFLECTION

This account is recorded in all three synoptic gospels. It contains many elements regarding deliverance from evil. Meeting evil's oppression in people can be somewhat scary, but we must remember that God is much more powerful than evil. This account points out at the beginning that no one was strong enough to subdue this man, and no chains could bind him. Yet Jesus bound and dismissed the evil spirits. Evil is no match for divine power. If in praying with someone we come upon a sense of evil being present, it is good to gather a group of believers to pray together while one person binds the power of evil in Jesus' name and sends it to the cross.

Rev. John Rice tells the story of how he was praying for a nun, sister Ruth. He writes,

> As I prayed, asking the Lord to show me how to pray for sister Ruth, I heard the Holy Spirit saying that her shoulder and neck pain was demonic in its origin. I resisted

The Gerasene Demoniac

praying for deliverance as I had never prayed this way before. The Lord persisted that this was how I was to pray. I then shared what I was hearing and asked Sr. Ruth if this made any sense to her. She quickly said yes, because her place of missionary work in South America was under the influence of a powerful witch doctor, who was known to speak darkness (curses) over members of her missionary team. I placed my hands on her and prayed not so very boldly, "If there is any demonic presence causing this pain in Sr. Ruth, in Jesus' name, I command you to release yourself from her and go to Jesus to be dealt with." Immediately, Sr. Ruth audibly gasped. She looked up at me and said. "I felt something leave and the pain is gone for the first time in two years." I realized that my ignorance and discomfort (fear) of praying in this way would have denied Sr. Ruth the healing she so yearned to receive, and that Jesus wanted to give.

It is crucial that we keep a balanced view of evil. Not all is evil, but evil is not just an intellectual concept. Jesus' power is stronger than evil, and he has given us authority in his name to bind and cast out evil if it oppresses a person or causes them pain. Jesus told his disciples, "I have given you authority to trample on snakes and scorpions and to overcome all the power of the enemy; nothing will harm you" (Luke 10:19). We must use his authority, or some people continue to suffer. It is important to be closely connected to Jesus, listen for his direction, and be obedient to him if we attempt to come against evil. We pray for healing first, and only if we or our team senses that there is something more do we consider binding any possible evil and sending it to the cross in Jesus' name. We may do this quietly. We must be careful not to tell a person they have evil in them when it may not be so. This can cause great fear and harm. If we pray to heal an emotional wound and the person is healed, any evil clinging to the wound often will leave. Sometimes, as we pray, a person will feel a force coming up through their throat and out of their mouth when an evil spirit is released as I described in the second healing account in this book.

Sometimes, it just leaves without any display. The person usually reports a release and a greater feeling of wellness afterward.

A good description of deliverance is loving someone out of spiritual darkness. We do not have to shout or be demonstrative. We pray for the presence of Jesus to come into the person and let his love cleanse them. In the nun's case, she did not choose evil. It was just trying to oppress her in her area of illness or woundedness. If a person has chosen to open themselves to evil through occult practices or a habitual unrepented sin, then they must want to get free. They must renew their commitment to Jesus and ask evil to leave. Those who pray with them support this choice in Jesus' name. The man in this gospel story came toward Jesus and fell on his knees. He wanted to be set free. One way of having people participate in their deliverances is to have them repeat their baptismal promises. They renounce evil and reclaim Jesus as the Lord of their life. Again, if you feel called to this ministry, I suggest you read Francis and Judith MacNutt's book, *Deliverance from Evil Spirits*.

We read that the demon knew Jesus and was fearful of Jesus. The presence of Jesus in you may aggravate an evil spirit troubling a person. They may feel more pain or sense that the pain is moving around. These are indications that deliverance is necessary to help them get well. After praying for healing, we would bind the spirit and command it in Jesus' name to leave. Then we would pray further inner healing prayers for the place where it had been residing.

We read that Jesus spoke directly to the demon. He does not converse with evil but only gets its name. Then he commands the evil to leave. We do the same. Knowing that we have the authority and the power from Jesus gives us peace about doing this ministry if needed. For most of my ministry, I focused on praying for inner healing, and often, evil left without any other prayers.

One interesting note I learned from a priest who did deliverance is that evil will leave quietly in the presence of the Eucharist. I often did ministry in church where the Eucharist was present.

The Jews believed that evil was in pigs and in the sea. That may be why the inclusion of pigs going into the sea is part of this story. It may refer to Isaiah chapter 65, verse four, were the evil

The Gerasene Demoniac

people lived among tombs and ate the flesh of swine. Whatever it is, we bind evil and send it to the cross.

This account ends with the once-possessed man sitting at the feet of Jesus, dressed and in his right mind. That is a description of being not only cured but made whole. He committed his life to Jesus. Once freed, the man needed inner healing and a connection to Jesus. His "sitting there dressed and in his right mind" describes this. He began to think the way Jesus thinks. He was clothed in Jesus' presence and accepted the teachings of Jesus. This is what "in his right mind" means. That is why Jesus could send him on mission back to his family to proclaim how much God had done for him. He was ready to talk about Jesus because he now had a faith relationship with Jesus. We are challenged to put on the mind of Jesus as the Apostle Paul says. We listen to Jesus' voice and speak as he directs. Once our mind and soul align with what Jesus desires for us, we are living in our right mind, which is the fullness of life.

The man could not come back with Jesus to the Jewish people because he would not have fit in. He had to go back to his people and proclaim the good news of healing and salvation. His new life would speak volumes to anyone who knew him before. He was in his right mind because he knew Jesus and the power of his love. He was thinking with divine thoughts. And that is why the people to whom he spoke were "amazed."

QUESTIONS TO PONDER/DISCUSS

- Why do you think Jesus ministers to this man who is not a Jew?
- Have you ever felt evil or been released from it?
- What do you think it would feel like to sit at the feet of Jesus and begin to connect your mind with his?
- What can we take away from this account?

PRACTICAL APPLICATION

Read through your baptismal promises and consider how important they are to keep you safe from the power of evil. Share, if you have a group, what they mean to you?

HEALING ACCOUNT 12

The Woman with a Hemorrhage

READ MARK 5:24B—34 (THIS ACCOUNT IS ALSO FOUND IN MATTHEW 9:20-22 AND LUKE 8:42-48)

24 A large crowd followed and pressed around Jesus. 25 And a woman was there who had been subject to bleeding for twelve years. 26 She had suffered a great deal under the care of many doctors and had spent all she had, yet instead of getting better she grew worse. 27 When she heard about Jesus, she came up behind him in the crowd and touched his cloak, 28 because she thought, "If I just touch his clothes, I will be healed." 29 Immediately her bleeding stopped and she felt in her body that she was freed from her suffering.

30 At once Jesus realized that power had gone out from him. He turned around in the crowd and asked, "Who touched my clothes?"

31 "You see the people crowding against you," his disciples answered, "and yet you can ask, 'Who touched me?'"

32 But Jesus kept looking around to see who had done it. 33 Then the woman, knowing what had happened to her, came and fell at his feet and, trembling with fear, told him the whole truth. 34 He said to her, "Daughter, your faith has healed you. Go in peace and be freed from your suffering."

REFLECTION

The account begins with the statement that a large crowd was following Jesus. Someone once said his greatest quality was his deep love and compassion for people. People were attracted to his overwhelming love. Our spiritual practices are meant to form us into people of great love and compassion. It is the foundation of the healing ministry and the call of the Christian life.

Because of the crowd, it was difficult to get to Jesus. We remember the four men who had to make a hole in the roof of the house to get their friend in the presence of Jesus. This woman had to push her way through the crowd. She had to get into the presence of Jesus. She had to push past the resistance. She had to do so knowing that in her culture, she was not supposed to touch anyone because they considered her unclean since she was bleeding. Imagine what she felt like as she pushed through the crowd. Her deep faith compelled her to find a way through the crowd. She was not just looking for a cure. She thinks that if she touches the garment of Jesus, she "will be healed." The word there (*sothesomai*) is not the word for "cured," but it is the word for "made whole." She already believed in Jesus, and she was going to stay connected to him. Once she felt the power of his presence, she fell at his feet as a gesture of worship. Now, she would be well forever. Before her cure, she believed in Jesus, but her faith connection got stronger after she touched him and received his healing love. I believe she had an experience of attachment love that I mentioned earlier.

This woman had to decide between religious propriety and actual need. She makes her choice because of her deep faith. Sometimes, we have to make a similar choice. Praying with someone for healing may not fit cultural norms of certain situations. Do we hold back or step forward and do what is necessary to proclaim Jesus' message of healing, forgiveness, and salvation? Jesus acted "outside the box" of his peers. Much of our healing ministry may be "outside the box," and that is often where the miraculous happens. We do not let the crowd we are in stop us from getting to Jesus. We cannot let distractions prevent us from "touching the

The Woman with a Hemorrhage

garment" of Jesus every day. That is the Christian journey. Take time to feel the power going out from him and then share it with those you meet.

This woman was also desperate. For twelve years, she had been bleeding and found no relief from any doctor. She put all her faith in Jesus. When I traveled to countries in Africa, the people there were much more open to healing through prayer than I had experienced here. They did not have the doctors like we do in America. Their last resort is Jesus, so they are open to receiving his healing love. They also take a lot of time to develop a close relationship with Jesus and trust that he will help them. This woman and many people in third-world countries model a deep, pure faith in Jesus. They challenge us to put our faith in him.

Jesus asks, "Who touched my clothes?" Many people touched him but only one touched him with faith-expectancy. Only one in the crowd expected to be radically healed and made whole through this touch. Jesus could tell that something was different about that touch. His response makes it clear that her faith had elicited power from him. That is the faith we need to carry on his healing ministry. We need to touch the presence of Jesus every day to be electrified with his love so that we can touch others in ministry with his healing. Jesus said to the woman, "Your faith has made you well." Again, it is the word for more than a cure. She had a new way of living and would be well forever.

Jesus also tells this woman to go in peace. We can imagine that she did not have too much peace living the way she did for twelve years. Now, she could live in the peace that only Jesus can give, the peace that the world does not know. Jesus promised his followers, "Peace I leave with you, my peace I give to you" (John 14:27). We can live in that peace by continuing a deep connection with Jesus. This woman, I believe, would follow him anywhere. Once she tasted his peace, she would remain with him for life. I would guess she was in the group of disciples with him as he went to Jerusalem to his death.

This woman's faith and willingness to push through the impossible can inspire us. She was not supposed to touch anyone because she would make them unclean. For her, to touch Jesus' garment was even more scary since he was a renowned teacher. Her belief gave her extraordinary courage. It sometimes takes extraordinary courage to reach out and pray with someone. We do not know their response, nor do we know what other people will think of us. We do not know what the person will say if nothing visible happens. But we push through our fears and bring the power of Jesus' love knowing, that if the person feels that love, something good will happen. Our faith is crucial in making that courageous journey.

If we understand the meaning of garments in the scripture, this story leaves us much on which to reflect. The garment in scripture represents the disposition of a person or their personality. If we "touch the personality of Jesus" every day, we can feel that healing anointing flow through us and be empowered to offer that gift to others. We push through other distractions that might keep us from daily prayer or weekly worship and take time to touch the garment of Jesus so that we are energized for the next healing encounter.

It is helpful, if we feel called to pray for someone, to invite the Holy Spirit to come into that encounter. We utterly depend on Jesus and the Holy Spirit to carry out the healing ministry in our world. Jesus uses people who are dependent on him to move in the world. He uses people who have been made well, who are born into a vibrant life with him, feeling his divine love every day. Without a connection to his power, we cannot set the atmosphere for miracles. Our surrendered hearts are a treasure to God because divine power is made tangible in the world today through our obedience to God. Within the swirl of God's power, we have true peace.

QUESTIONS TO PONDER/DISCUSS

- Do you ever feel energy draining out of you? Where do you get revitalized?
- Why did Jesus heal the way he did in this account?

The Woman with a Hemorrhage

- What do you think it felt like to be that woman or someone who knew her?
- What are the messages of this account?

PRACTICAL APPLICATION

Imagine being right in front of Jesus. Touch his garment, his hands. Look into his eyes. Share with someone what you are feeling. Invite someone to do the same. Talk with them about what they felt when they did this also.

HEALING ACCOUNT 13

Jairus' Daughter

READ MARK 5:21-24, 35-43 (THIS ACCOUNT IS ALSO RECORDED IN MATTHEW 9:18-19, 23-26 AND LUKE 8:40-42, 49-56)

21 When Jesus had again crossed over by boat to the other side of the lake, a large crowd gathered around him while he was by the lake. 22 Then one of the synagogue rulers, named Jairus, came there. Seeing Jesus, he fell at his feet 23 and pleaded earnestly with him, "My daughter is dying. Please come and put your hands on her so that she will be healed and live. 24 So Jesus went with him . . .

35 While Jesus was still speaking some men came from the house of Jairus, the synagogue ruler. "Your daughter is dead," they said. "Why bother the teacher anymore?"

36 Ignoring what they said, Jesus told the synagogue ruler, "Don't be afraid; just believe."

37 He did not let anyone follow him except Peter, James, and John the brother of James. 38 When they came to the home of the synagogue ruler, Jesus saw a commotion, with people crying and wailing loudly. 39 He went in and said to them, "Why all the commotion and wailing? The child is not dead but asleep." 40 But they laughed at him.

After he put them all out, he took the child's father and mother and the disciples who were with him, and went in where the child was. 41 He took her by the hand and said to her, *"Talitha koum!"* (which means, "Little girl, I say to you, get up!"). 42 Immediately the girl stood up and walked around (she was twelve years old). At this they were completely astonished. 43 He gave strict orders not to let anyone know about this, and told them to give her something to eat.

REFLECTION

Here, we read the account wrapped around the story of the woman with the hemorrhage. Both accounts describe people of great faith in Jesus. They understand the need to be closely connected to Jesus. The woman believed she could be made whole, and this synagogue ruler is asking for the same thing for his daughter. His falling at the feet of Jesus indicates his submission to Jesus, and he requests that his daughter will "be healed and live." He is asking that she not only be made whole but that she will have "life." This is the same word describing the centurion's son in our first account, who not only was cured but was given life. The Greek word for this is *Zoë*. It is the kind of life we can have with a deep committed connection to Jesus and a submission to his will. It is a transformed life lived in his presence every day.

After this ruler makes his request for his daughter, Jesus gets delayed by the woman with the hemorrhage. Jesus is not concerned about being delayed because he knows his power is strong enough to give healing and to give life. Because he was held up, this man's friends came to him with the news that his daughter had already died. Jesus tells the man not to be afraid but to continue to believe. When we pray with people, sometimes the results get delayed. God's timing may be different than our desires. Trusting in God's goodness and deep love allows us to stay in the peace of the divine presence. We keep believing that God ultimately gives us the fullness of life if we stay connected. As healing ministers, we encourage people to remain connected to Jesus, trusting his promise of Life.

When Jesus got to the room where the daughter was, he assured the people that the girl was not dead. Her father believed that Jesus would give her life. The people laughed at Jesus. We may experience that kind of response from some people, maybe even our peers when we offer to minister healing prayer, but like Jesus, we do it anyway. We do not run from the pain of ridicule but rather give people hope in the Life-giver.

When Dr. Chauncey Crandall, who I mentioned earlier, went back into the emergency room and asked the doctor to minister the shock one more time after the patient was dead for forty-five minutes, he received some resistance and ridicule from the ER doctor. He told him to do it any way, and the man came back to life. He heard the voice of Jesus telling him that this man was to have life. When we pray, we may hear our voices on the inside telling us that this won't work or that we will look foolish, but we must push past those voices and do it anyway if God has called us to do it. Even if we do not get the result that we want, we know that if we bring the healing love of Jesus to an encounter, some level of healing always happens. If we give in to the resistance, someone continues to suffer. Many Christians have done that for too long, and now we are called to change the tide and return to doing what Jesus did, what he has called us to do. We can give people the hope to "get well and live." We must stand firm in faith and do whatever Jesus tells us.

When Jesus got to the room where the girl was, it said, "he put them all out." He wanted to create an atmosphere of openness to his healing power. When we pray with people, to create an environment of belief and openness to Jesus' love and his desire to heal is helpful. We bring the positive energy of his healing love, and it is appropriate to clear away any noise or people who do not foster that environment. Having a time of praise and worship, together with reading and speaking God's word, can often help create this God-centered atmosphere, where the powerful energy of the Holy Spirit can move freely to bring healing and new life.

This account is about life. It tells us the ultimate purpose of Jesus' ministry. He came that we could be forgiven of our sins, healed of the sins done to us, and receive the fullness of life in him. It is a precious gift that he did not have to give except that his heart is moved with compassion for each of us, and he does not want us to live in pain or be disconnected from the Father. He wants to raise us to real life, in union with our creator. We are called to offer that life to the people we meet.

One extra note in this account is that Mark includes the Aramaic words that Jesus would have used. He writes, "Jesus said to her, '*Talitha koum*' (which means, 'Little girl, I say to you, get up'")." This assures us of the credibility of this story and the stories in Mark's gospel. It tells us the healings of Jesus are undeniable. It gives us the courage to continue what he did. The more we learn his ways, the more we can carry out his ministry.

QUESTIONS TO PONDER/DISCUSS

- Have you ever fallen at the feet of Jesus and submitted your whole heart and will to him? If so, what did it feel like?
- How can you prepare yourself and create an atmosphere for healing?
- What fears or resistance do you have to push through to do healing ministry?
- What can we take away from this healing account?

PRACTICAL APPLICATION

The account says the people laughed at Jesus when he said the girl was asleep. Is there any part of your life or ministry that has been stifled because of the ridicule of others? Ask someone to pray with you for Jesus to bring new life to that areas. Feel him with you to step past the ridicule and live as Jesus desires.

HEALING ACCOUNT 14

Two Blind Men

READ MATTHEW 9:27-31

27 As Jesus went on from there, two blind men followed him, calling out, "Have mercy on us, Son of David!"
28 When he had gone indoors, the blind men came to him, and he asked them, "Do you believe that I am able to do this?"
"Yes, Lord," they replied.
29 Then he touched their eyes and said, "According to your faith will it be done to you," 30 and their sight was restored. Jesus warned them sternly, "See that no one knows about this." 31 But they went out and spread the news about him all over the region.

REFLECTION

This account is similar to one we will explore in Mark's gospel later when we explore miracle number 18. There are a couple of things we can glean from this account.

Jesus pulls away from the crowd in this story and goes indoors. It is hard to tell why he does that, but he may have wanted to speak with the men more privately. This is one story where Jesus asks if they have faith in him. We have seen that the ones who

Two Blind Men

receive healing need to be open to the healing power of Jesus. With that openness, Jesus could bring about a cure.

At the end of this healing account, Jesus said to the men who had received their sight, "See that no one knows about this." This tells us that they had not yet made a faith commitment to Jesus. They only saw the physical cure rather than the fullness of life that Jesus offers to all who enter a faith relationship with him. They were not yet "made well." They would only "see" the real purpose of life when they surrendered their life to him. He asked them to be quiet because they did not yet know the full message that he was bringing to the world. When we proclaim the message of Jesus, it is important that we have the complete message that he spoke. I have summarized this message in my book, *Living a Transformed Life—The Core of Christianity*.

The account in John 9:1–38 describes a blind man who now "sees," and did make a faith commitment to Jesus. This cure did not get to that level, but it is significant as it may have been the one step that would eventually lead to life in Jesus. Each of our encounters done in Jesus' name moves a person along their journey to a faith relationship with Jesus. It may take many encounters in one's life, but if we do our part, the person will be ready for their next spiritual encounter. The healing ministry is a big part of bringing people to know the fullness of life in Jesus.

Jesus' healing ministry was significant in verifying his teaching that he wanted people to be well. It also invites people to consider a deep relationship with him. It is vital that we, as Christians, use this gift of healing to proclaim the power of Jesus' love and his desire to make people well. It is an integral part of inviting people to see their purpose in life and discover what life is really about. We are part of a divine mission, and our faith in Jesus makes it possible.

QUESTIONS TO PONDER/DISCUSS

- How have you opened your eyes to the divine purpose for your life?
- How are you preparing yourself to understand and proclaim the full message of Jesus?
- What methods does Jesus use to bring about healing?
- What can we learn from this story?

PRACTICAL APPLICATION

Jesus went indoors and talked with the blind men. Take some time to go into your private prayer place and talk with Jesus about his purpose and destiny for your life.

HEALING ACCOUNT 15

The Mute, Possessed Man

READ MATTHEW 9:32-34

32 While they were going out, a man who was demon-possessed and could not talk was brought to Jesus. 33 And when the demon was driven out, the man who had been mute spoke. The crowd was amazed and said, "Nothing like this has ever been seen in Israel."
34 But the Pharisees said, "It is by the prince of demons that he drives out demons."

REFLECTION

We have read about Jesus driving out demons in previous stories. This account does not describe the deliverance but states that it happened. What we notice is that once delivered, the mute man could speak. Severe trauma can cause a person to stutter or be unable to speak. Evil can cling to serious inner wounds. Praying for healing may involve taking Jesus to the core of the presenting problem and freeing a person in Jesus' name from a lingering evil force. In the name of Jesus, we can do this important ministry.

This account of Jesus driving out a demon ends in a very unique and interesting way. In response to this miracle, the Pharisees said, "It is by the prince of demons that he drives out demons."

This attitude is what Jesus will later describe as the "sin against the Holy Spirit," which is to attribute to some lesser force what comes only from God. Instead of praising God for this miracle, they stayed imprisoned in their false assumption. The man who had been bound was freed, and those who thought they were free were bound by their unwillingness to accept Jesus. It is important that we give the glory and praise to God for the many ways God demonstrates the power of divine love in our lives and the lives of others. No other power can bring people the fullness of life.

One challenge of the healing ministry is to keep the focus on God. It is not our power that makes these things happen. We are only vessels who carry the treasure of God's love. People often thank me when a healing occurs, but I quickly invite them to thank God. It is not luck that someone is miraculously healed. Certain things might be luck, but when we see the movement of God change an illness or restore life, we must give credit to our Maker. Medicine can help with illnesses, but when the restoration of health is beyond medicine, we must attribute the result to God. When a person releases a painful memory and even the evil that clings to it, then a counselor knows that something happened beyond their capabilities. Remember to praise God for these kinds of healings so that the people involved keep their eyes fixed on the source of the transforming power.

The people's response to this miracle is very telling. In scripture, when people are "amazed," something divine happened. They never saw anything like it because no one ever brought the presence of God to earth like Jesus did. No one carried the divine, creative love and authoritative power as Jesus did. To the extent that we carry that love and use divine authority, we can do things many people have never seen before. That is our mission given to us by Jesus.

QUESTIONS TO PONDER/DISCUSS

- How might you pray for someone who has difficulty with speech?
- Why do you think the Pharisees attribute Jesus' divine power to demons?
- Have you dealt with people who attribute healings to something other than God?
- What can we glean from this short account?

PRACTICAL APPLICATION

Break into groups of two. Have one person receive prayer while the other prays that God would give them the courage and the vocabulary to proclaim the gospel. Pray for freedom from anything that holds them back from speaking about Jesus with conviction. When finished, switch roles.

HEALING ACCOUNT 16

The Daughter of the Canaanite Woman

READ MARK 7:24-30 (THIS ACCOUNT IS ALSO FOUND IN MATTHEW 15:21-28)

24 Jesus left that place and went to the vicinity of Tyre. He entered a house and did not want anyone to know it, yet he could not keep his presence secret. 25 In fact, as soon as she heard about him, a woman whose little daughter was possessed by an evil spirit came and fell at his feet. 26 The woman was a Greek, born in Syrian Phoenicia. She begged Jesus to drive the demon out of her daughter.

27 "First let the children eat all they want," he told her, "for it is not right to take the children's bread and toss it to the dogs."

28 "Yes, Lord," she replied, "but even the dogs under the table eat the children's crumbs."

29 Then he told her, "For such a reply, you may go; the demon has left your daughter."

30 She went home and found her child lying on the bed, and the demon gone.

The Daughter of the Canaanite Woman

REFLECTION

The context of this account is that Jesus had been ministering in Galilee and was tired. To get a rest, he went off to Tyre, which is in Gentile territory. Even though he tried to stay unnoticed, this woman still found him. Jesus could not find rest. As ministers of healing, if we help many people, we may get in a similar situation. Sometimes, we must offer Jesus' healing love when we are tired. If we are not trying to do it from our power but just allowing the healing love of Jesus to flow through us, it does not take too much energy. We surrender to whatever Jesus asks of us. Jesus gives us times when we can rest. We need to receive those times and allow ourselves to be refreshed for the next encounter.

This woman was a non-Jew. Jesus felt called to "feed" the children of Israel first. Interestingly, he had just fed five thousand who were Jews, and there was bread left over. Everyone would eventually be able to eat from the table of life. The Acts of the Apostle tells us how the early Christians concluded that they had to invite non-Jews to share in baptism and the life of Jesus.

The bantering between the woman and Jesus indicates that there would be enough food for the "dogs" as well. In that culture, the gentiles were referred to as dogs. Jesus uses normal language but a milder diminutive, calling them "pups." It indicates his sensitivity in this dialogue. These pups were allowed under the table. To feed the pups while the family was eating was inappropriate: they would be fed after the children had eaten. This understanding enables the woman to point out that even the little pets under the table can have crumbs that fall on the floor. The dialogue between Jesus and the woman may seem offensive to us, but it was the usual bantering of the time. Through it, Jesus ascertained whether the woman had a certain faith for this request. Once Jesus assesses her openness to his power, he grants the deliverance and healing for her daughter.

This story is very significant in the early church's decision to take the message of Jesus to the Gentiles. They recognized that even though Jesus' initial mission began with the Jews, he showed that he also would offer healing and salvation to the Gentiles. The woman indicates the Gentile's desire and readiness to receive Jesus' love and message. This story proclaims that we are called to minister Jesus' love to everyone. There are no limits. To those who receive it, there is the hope of wholeness and new life.

In this story, we read how the woman fell at the feet of Jesus, which is a sign of respect. It carries a connotation of worship, indicating that this woman was ready to enter into a faith relationship with Jesus. She was willing to surrender to his will. She acknowledged her dependence on God. People often open themselves to God when illness occurs or death comes near. Healing prayer gives us a chance to use those opportunities to invite them to a life-giving relationship with their Maker.

We might note that the Canaanites sacrificed to other gods. They even did child sacrifices and other vile practices. They opened themselves to evil. There are people today who do similar things, getting involved in voodoo and occult practices. I heard a story of three children committing suicide. It was found out later that this tragedy was related to their grandmother's involvement in voodoo. If we run into situations like this, we need at least to be aware of what might be happening and, if possible gather a team that could help offer healing and freedom. With Jesus' power, we can bind and dispel evil and pray for healing.

Again, we see that Jesus' power to heal and deliver can flow over a distance. He did not even get near the girl and she was freed and healed. Our prayers from a distance or over the phone can be effective because Jesus' power is not limited by geography. Our connection with him and our ability to communicate his love to another person are the key elements in healing others.

QUESTIONS TO PONDER/DISCUSS

- What is the cultural context of this encounter? How does it inform us about Jesus' healing ministry?
- Self-care is important for us, but sometimes we must do ministry when we are tired. Can you describe a time like that?

- Have you ever ministered to someone outside of your normal social relationships?
- What can we take from this account?

PRACTICAL APPLICATION

When you go to your church, make it a point to talk with someone outside your normal group. Listen to their concerns and see if there is any area where they need healing. If you feel Jesus calling you to address their need, offer to pray with them.

HEALING ACCOUNT 17
Deaf Man with a Speech Impediment

READ MARK 7:31-37

31 Then Jesus left the vicinity of Tyre and went through Sidon, down to the Sea of Galilee and into the region of the Decapolis. 32 There some people brought to him a man who was deaf and could hardly talk, and they begged him to place his hands on the man.

33 After he took him aside, away from the crowd, Jesus put his finger into the man's ears. Then he spit and touched the man's tongue. 34 He looked up to heaven and with a deep sigh said to him, "*Ephphatha!*" (which means, "Be opened!"). 35 At this, the man's ears were opened, his tongue was loosened and he began to speak plainly.

36 Jesus commanded them not to tell anyone. But the more he did so, the more they kept talking about it. 37 People were overwhelmed with amazement. "He has done everything well," they said. "He makes the deaf hear and the mute speak."

REFLECTION

In this account, we see something that we have seen before. People bring this man to Jesus with the hope of healing. It is interesting,

Deaf Man with a Speech Impediment

however, that Jesus takes the man away from that group of people to minister healing. It seems Jesus wanted a quiet atmosphere of love for his healing presence to flow as the crowd did not provide an environment for healing. Jesus creates an environment away from the crowd. Sometimes, we may need a quiet space to listen to a person and offer healing prayer. We create a spot most conducive to bathing a person in Jesus' love.

We also notice that Jesus did not do what they asked. They asked Jesus to place his hands on the man, but Jesus chose a different method for this healing. Each situation is unique, and Jesus knew what was needed for this healing to occur. His method here is unique. Jesus' gestures are sacramental in that they affect what they symbolize. They open the man's ears and loose his tongue to speak.

I recall an incident where a woman received her hearing during a large Eucharist service in Belgium. After sharing in the praise and receiving communion, this woman began to hear. She came forward all excited because the bones of her ears had been removed long ago, and since then, she could not hear. On this day, during the worship, her hearing was restored. We did not specifically pray for her or touch her ears. God moves in many ways. What seems important is that we create atmospheres in which people can experience healing and new life in God's love.

We might wonder about Jesus spitting and then touching the man's tongue. In his book, *Mark—Good News for Hard Times*, George Montague writes, "In our highly antiseptic culture, communication by spittle is regarded as offensive. In Jesus' day, it was highly esteemed as an instrument of healing. There is a physical communication, via spittle, from the tongue of Jesus to the bound tongue of the man." We may sometimes use oil to anoint someone or place our hand on the place of pain, or share communion with them. These sacramental gestures can convey God's love and desire to heal. Transmitting Jesus' healing love can be done in many ways. We listen to Jesus' direction and do what he directs.

Jesus "looked up to heaven" and then prayed. This is a sign of his close relationship with *Abba*. That close connection empowers him to heal. He then said, *Ephphatha*, which means "be opened."

Jesus' word, *Ephphatha*, encompasses not only the request to open the man's ears but also for him to be open and hear all that God has in mind for him. Jesus' healing ministry always had the deeper goal of making a person whole by bringing them into a faith relationship with him. This informs us of our mission in the healing ministry. We might note that Mark's use of the original Aramaic word that Jesus would have used again shows us the authenticity and the reliability of this story.

We read how Jesus asked the crowd not to tell anyone of this event. They saw the cure but were not ready to proclaim who Jesus was. They had not made a commitment to follow him. They were amazed at the cure but unable to feel the richer life that Jesus came to give.

The last verse alludes to the words of the prophet Isaiah. They proclaimed that when the Jews would return from exile, God would bless them with new life. Part of the restoration was that "the eyes of the blind will be opened and the ears of the deaf unstopped. Then will the lame leap like a deer, and the mute tongue shout for joy" (Isaiah 35:5–6). Jesus was bringing about a whole new restoration. His healing ministry was awakening new life and new hope for the people of his time. When we minister his healing love, we convey this same message of hope and the promise of eternal life found in Jesus.

The man in the account was not quite ready to evangelize, but if he kept listening, he would one day know the joy of a life-giving relationship with Jesus. He was one step closer to having his mouth free to speak the gospel. When we hear what God is saying to us and are open to his direction, we are free to speak of his amazing love.

QUESTIONS TO PONDER/DISCUSS

- How did the crowd assist in the healing? How did they hamper the healing?
- Have you ever seen someone's hearing restored or a speech impediment healed?

Deaf Man with a Speech Impediment

- How can we help open the ears of people to the healing and saving message of Jesus?
- What can we learn about healing from this story?

PRACTICAL APPLICATION

Ask if anyone in your group or you know has a physical pain or trouble hearing or speaking. Listen to how God would like you to pray, and then pray for the person as directed.

HEALING ACCOUNT 18

The Blind Man at Bethsaida

READ MARK 8:22–26

22 They came to Bethsaida, and some people brought a blind man and begged Jesus to touch him. 23 He took the blind man by the hand and led him outside the village. When he had spit on the man's eyes and put his hands on him, Jesus asked, "Do you see anything?"

24 He looked up and said, "I see people; they look like trees walking around."

25 Once more Jesus put his hands on the man's eyes. Then his eyes were opened, his sight was restored, and he saw everything clearly. 26 Jesus sent him home, saying, "Don't go into the village."

REFLECTION

In this healing account, we again read of a group of people bringing a man to Jesus. We do not know if the man knew Jesus or had faith in him. It seems the people had faith that Jesus could cure this man. These people are like us, who bring people into Jesus' presence for healing. We recognize that our role as Christians and healing ministers is to bring people into the presence of Jesus. Sometimes, we may be able to use worship music to invite people to feel the presence of Jesus. We used to sing spiritual music before every communion service. One woman who was present during that time told me after the service that the pain in her knees was healed as we sang God's praises. Another woman said that after she relieved communion, she felt like a blanket of love was over her, and filling her with a deep peace. These events are powerful times to soak people in God's healing love.

If we are alone, we can set an atmosphere for healing by welcoming a person and attentively listening to their concern. By assuring them of God's love, we can create a place for them to receive healing. Our prayers may speak of God's love and let them know God's desire to heal them. Appropriate gentle touch can transmit Jesus' healing energy. Looking at people with love and care may help bring them into the presence of Jesus. The main thing is that we bring the person seeking healing into an awareness of his deep love for them. Reading one of these healing stories may open them to his power and desire to heal them.

This particular account is unique in that it is the only recorded time when the person Jesus was ministering to was not healed right away. Jesus used spit again, as we saw in the last account, but putting it on the man's eyes did not bring about a total cure. The man could see but only partially. Then Jesus repeated his ministry to his eyes, and the man could see clearly.

This unique story demonstrates several things about the healing ministry. First, we see that Jesus asked the man if he saw anything. It is appropriate when praying with someone to ask them what is happening. We may inquire if their pain is lessening or changing. Second, we also read that when the man was not totally healed, Jesus prayed again. It is important to note that we can pray a number of times for a person. Sometimes, a second prayer brings a healing and sometimes, we need to continue soaking a person in prayer for a long time. Repeated prayer can soak out deep pains and diseases, bringing healing and new life. Soaking prayer is powerful to dispel difficult diseases and cleanse inner wounds. There is no limit to what can happen when we soak a person in Jesus' healing love. Praying for a long time or repeated prayers for a person is in keeping with the ministry of Jesus.

One man who came for the healing of his cancer asked us to pray for him. He was starting chemo treatments and wanted us to pray that those treatments would not have side effects and that they would do what they were meant to do. He came each week for six weeks before each of his treatments. He did not have any side effects from his treatments, and at the end of the six weeks, he was cancer-free.

We prayed healing prayers every week at our church community during our Sunday service right after people received communion. It was a very powerful time for people to receive healing. Church communities would benefit greatly from this practice. People felt the love of Jesus during those services, and many experienced gradual healings and a new awareness of the love of God. Sometimes, we call this soaking prayer. It can be done individually or in a group. One woman came with ovarian cancer. The community soaked her and her husband in prayer for several weeks. She made some changes in her life and committed her life to Jesus. They did treatments to shrink the cancer and then eventually did surgery to remove it. When they opened her up, the cancer was completely gone. In addition to the physical healing, she discovered a whole new life in Jesus.

Healing prayer is not contrary to the use of medicine or counseling. The two go together. We have found that often prayer helps the medicine work more effectively. One doctor said that after surgery, his patients only needed one-third of the normal pain medication when his staff also prayed with them for healing. It is wonderful to see that many health-care professionals recognize the healing benefits of prayer in their practice. Counselors have found the same thing. Often, these are situations of soaking prayer, and they produce remarkable results. There is an organization of professional health-care people called ACTHeals. Its members pray with their patients and encourage this practice among their peers. This group can be found at www.actheals.org.

This scripture account is encouraging for prayer ministers who do not see immediate results. It is important not to be discouraged but to continue to soak a person in God's love. When we

The Blind Man at Bethsaida

do this, something good always happens. Sometimes, it leads to a new insight or a life change. Sometimes, it releases the pain. Sometimes, it brings a feeling of peace and joy to the person. We prayed with one woman during the evening service at a retreat. The next morning, we asked what people had experienced. She said, "My arthritis still hurts some, but I don't care anymore because I feel so loved by Jesus. His presence in my heart is much more important." We love with the love of Jesus and pray as Jesus directs. The results are in his hands.

QUESTIONS TO PONDER/DISCUSS

- Why did Jesus minister healing the way he did?
- How have you brought people into the presence of Jesus?
- How might you help someone open their eyes to the love Jesus has for them?
- What can we take from this account?

PRACTICAL APPLICATION

If you have a group, have one-half of the people sit on a row of chairs, and the other half stand behind each of them, gently lay their hands on the person, and soak them in prayer for an extended time. Then, switch roles. Share what you felt. If you are alone, go to someone in need and ask if you may soak them in prayer.

HEALING ACCOUNT 19

The Epileptic Boy

READ MARK 9:14-28 (THIS ACCOUNT IS ALSO FOUND IN MATTHEW 17:14-20 AND LUKE 9:37-43)

14 When they came to the other disciples, they saw a large crowd around them and the teachers of the law arguing with them. 15 As soon as all the people saw Jesus, they were overwhelmed with wonder and ran to greet him.

16 "What are you arguing with them about?" he asked.

17 A man in the crowd answered, "Teacher, I brought you my son, who is possessed by a spirit that has robbed him of speech. 18 Whenever it seizes him, it throws him to the ground. He foams at the mouth, gnashes his teeth and becomes rigid. I asked your disciples to drive out the spirit, but they could not."

19 "O unbelieving generation," Jesus replied, "How long shall I stay with you? How long shall I put up with you? Bring the boy to me."

20 So they brought him. When the spirit saw Jesus, it immediately threw the boy into a convulsion. He fell to the ground and rolled around, foaming at the mouth.

21 Jesus asked the boy's father, "How long has he been like this?"

"From childhood," he answered. 22 "It has often thrown him into fire or water to kill him. But if you can

The Epileptic Boy

do anything, take pity on us and help us." 23 "'If you can'?" said Jesus. "Everything is possible for him who believes."

24 Immediately the boy's father exclaimed, "I do believe; help me overcome my unbelief!"

25 When Jesus saw that a crowd was running to the scene, he rebuked the evil spirit. "You deaf and mute spirit," he said, "I command you, come out of him and never enter him again."

26 The spirit shrieked, convulsed him violently and came out. The boy looked so much like a corpse that many said, "He's dead." 27 But Jesus took him by the hand and lifted him to his feet, and he stood up.

28 After Jesus had gone indoors, his disciples asked him privately, "Why couldn't we drive it out?"

29 He replied, "This kind can come out only by prayer."

REFLECTION

The setting of this account is Jesus coming down the mountain after being Transfigured. Peter, James, and John were with him. Together, they come to the crowd and find out that a man had brought his son for deliverance and healing, and the disciples who did not go up the mountain could not deliver and heal the boy. It must have been discouraging for them. At times, we may get discouraged if we do not see results from our prayer for healing. What is important is that we do not give up. The best thing we can do is to seek to deepen our relationship with Jesus. Taking more time to absorb his love and consciously be in his presence puts our hearts at peace and fills us with more strength to offer healing. We may also try to discern the core issue and take Jesus to that place.

Jesus' comment about an unbelieving generation does not seem to fit in this story. It may be a later addition. What we notice is that when Jesus got close to the spirit, it became agitated. The evil spirit cannot stand being by Jesus. In Uganda, when we started praising God, a number of participants felt a spirit causing disruption inside them. We bound the spirit and commanded it to leave. The spirits left. We do not dialogue with an evil spirit but command it with the authority of Jesus.

The disciples were unable to do this on this occasion. They did not seem connected to Jesus' power as they had earlier. Jesus tells them later that this kind of spirit can only come out by prayer. I believe he was talking about the prayer preparation that is needed to be empowered to do healing and deliverance. Remember, Jesus had just been up the mountain praying to the Father with such depth that his clothes lit up. He was transfigured. He tells his disciples that their preparation for this ministry involves being deeply connected to the divine, supernatural energy. We receive this same message. Healing ministry requires a consistent spirituality of listening to Jesus, honoring him, and surrendering to his will.

The father in this story recognizes that his belief in Jesus is not very strong, but he prays for a deeper faith. He needed a greater faith connection to Jesus so that Jesus' healing power could flow through him to his son. We saw this in the healing of the royal official's son (John 4:46–54). No matter the person's faith for whom we pray, we bring our faith relationship with Jesus to every encounter. If it has diminished, we need to examine what we are doing and make changes to strengthen our relationship with Jesus. Having a healing community like those of the Order of St. Luke or ACTHeals, can help keep our faith life alive, overflowing with the love of Jesus. Jesus said the living water he gives will become "a fountain within us leaping up to provide eternal life." When we are deeply connected, his love is like a fountain that flows through us and over us to bring healing.

Perhaps one of the biggest blocks to healing today is the unbelief in our culture and even in some of our churches. Many people have forgotten that Jesus' healing power is available to us. Some religious teachers have taught that Jesus does not heal today and never did, even when he was on earth. We must stand against the disbelief in our generation and proclaim the power of Jesus' healing love. Many people continue to suffer because Christians do not carry out Jesus' commission to heal the sick and dispel evil. We have the authority to continue to do what Jesus did.

The Epileptic Boy

We might take a moment to consider the emotional healing that Jesus did for this man. He must have been stressed out if he had lived with his son for a long time. He lived in fear of losing his son. Jesus brings comfort to this man's heart by healing his son. Often, the healing ministry touches a number of lives and brings peace and new hope to the whole network of relationships.

QUESTIONS TO PONDER/DISCUSS

- Do you ever feel like you do not have enough power to pray with someone for healing? How can you change that?
- What do you think the father in the account did after his encounter with Jesus?
- Does your church often offer prayers for healing? How might you make it happen?
- What elements of healing and deliverance can we glean from this account?

PRACTICAL APPLICATION

Talk with each other about how you plan to stay alive in your faith and avoid discouragement when healings do not happen as you hoped.

HEALING ACCOUNT 20

The Woman Caught in Adultery

READ JOHN 8:1-11

1 Jesus went to the Mount of Olives. 2 At dawn he appeared again in the temple court, where all the people gathered around him, and he sat down to teach them. 3 The teachers of the law and the Pharisees brought in a woman caught in adultery. They made her stand before the group 4 and said to Jesus, "Teacher, this woman was caught in the act of adultery. 5 In the Law Moses commanded us to stone such women. Now what do you say?" 6 They were using this question as a trap, in order to have a basis for accusing him.

But Jesus bent down and started to write on the ground with his finger. 7 When they kept questioning him, he straightened up and said to them, "If any one of you is without sin, let him be the first to throw a stone at her." 8 Again he stooped down and wrote on the ground.

9 At this, those who heard began to go away one at a time, the older ones first, until only Jesus was left, with the woman still standing there. 10 Jesus straightened up and asked her, "Woman, where are they? Has no one condemned you?"

11 "No one, sir," she said.

"Then neither do I condemn you," Jesus declared. "Go now and leave your life of sin."

The Woman Caught in Adultery

REFLECTION

In this account, we read about an interesting encounter. We might wonder how it fits the category of a healing account, but when we look deeper, we notice people living with some inner wounds and destructive ways. Jesus was teaching the people with his words, and then he taught them by how he responded to this situation. Jesus demonstrates the power of divine love that gives new life rather than taking a life. It shows a new way of relating. It demonstrates his desire to have us live in unity with his plan for us.

The scene was Jerusalem, where the teachers of the law and the Pharisees were carrying out a practice that they felt was in keeping with the law of Moses. Jesus demonstrated a picture of the "new Moses," who offers a life-giving law empowered by divine love and forgiveness. His actions and words show a different way of handling the spiritual destruction of behaviors that defile a person. He offers the power to change.

Jesus does not condemn the woman for her behavior, but he does call her to "leave her life of sin." Apparently, this was an ongoing pattern in her life, and Jesus wanted to free her from that pattern. He did what the stones could not do. He challenged her to make a life change. His love for her was not enabling her destructive behavior. His acceptance of her did not condone or accept what she was doing but gave her a way out of the web of destructive relationships. We can reflect on the core wound within her that caused her to live a "life of sin." By loving this woman with true love and calling her to change her behavior, Jesus offered her a life of wholeness and inner peace. This account is similar to Jesus healing the woman at the well (John 4:4–42). She, too, was caught in a web of destructive relationships, and through a healing dialogue with Jesus, she was able to heal, change, and be free.

This powerful healing account offers a unique model of healing the core issues of a person caught in the life style of destructive behavior. Jesus' response to this woman shows a way between just "stoning" such a person or just condoning their destructive behavior. Neither of those responses is life-giving or healing. In our world, people often offer one or the other of those responses, but Jesus offers a healing response. His love ministers to the inner wound that causes the destructive behavior. As Christians and ministers of healing, we are challenged to respond to people in the same way and offer his life-giving gift to set them free. If we truly love people as Jesus did, we will not condemn a person but seek a way of inviting them to experience Jesus' deep love for them. We also will not pretend to "love" them when, in fact, we are enabling them to remain in their destructive lifestyle. That is not loving. Loving them as Jesus did offers the power and the challenge to change. Those who accept it can be transformed and healed.

We might also reflect on what Jesus offers to the teachers of the law and the Pharisees. He says to them, *"Let the man among you who has no sin be the first to cast a stone at her."* (New American translation) The fact is they were all men bringing this woman. We wonder why this group of all men who catch a woman in the act of adultery have such a need to kill her. And why don't they bring the man who was *"caught in the act of adultery"*? He must have been there. They said it is their law to stone her, but why do they hold to that law so firmly when they disregard other laws? What is really going on here? Their response to Jesus' statement tells us that they were in denial of their own sin. They try to get rid of the woman so they do not have to deal with the sin in their own lives. Rather than dealing with their own behavior, they project their unrepented sin on this woman. How often had they committed adultery either physically or in their mind? There wasn't a man among them who was ready to stand up, call them to be honest about their own sin, and challenge them to change. The law gave them an excuse to live in their denial. Jesus calls them to honestly take a moral inventory. Jesus may have offended them, but his words offered them a chance to get free of their destructive behavior and live as he modeled. His response provided them a chance for repentance, forgiveness, healing, and transformation. They walked away with something to think about.

This account shows the unequal dynamics between men and women in Jesus' time. Jesus affirms the equal dignity of women and men. We can also read that in his teachings about marriage (Mark 10:2–12). This is a cultural healing. Jesus challenged their law and their practices which opened the way for men and woman to care for each other and connect in a deeper way. Each could experience the joy and energy of being a daughter or son of *Abba*. Then, they would treat each other as part of the divine family. As Christians in the healing ministry, we are called to demonstrate this healing way of relating, empowered by our true identity in Jesus. This is a healing story of a different type, but it is an important one for our culture today.

We have seen how Jesus' healing ministry not only cured some people but offered them the fullness of life. In this account, we see Jesus offering the fullness of life, which is found in healing the deep inner wounds that cause people to live a "life of sin." Modeling what Jesus did in this account means we must take time to soak in his love to such a degree that we can respond in a similar way to these types of situations. We must be radically honest with ourselves and seek to change any destructive behavior in our lives. We need to look at core wounds that may be at the base of such behavior. If we make this spiritual and inner healing journey, then we can invite other people on this freeing journey as well.

QUESTIONS TO PONDER/DISCUSS

- What do you think the woman was feeling as she met Jesus?
- What response would she have expected? What did Jesus' response do for her?
- How might we bring this type of healing to our culture or to our churches?
- What can we take away from this healing account?

PRACTICAL APPLICATION

Do a moral inventory and seek to honestly name any things in your attitudes or behavior that do not align with Jesus' message. If necessary, make a sincere repentance. Then, seek to respond to people the way Jesus did.

HEALING ACCOUNT 21

The Man Born Blind

READ JOHN 9:1-38

1 As Jesus went along, he saw a man blind from birth. 2 His disciples asked him, "Rabbi, who sinned, this man or his parents, that he was born blind?"

3 "Neither this man nor his parents sinned." said Jesus, "but this happened so that the works of God might be displayed in his life. 4 As long as it is day, we must do the works of him who sent me. Night is coming, when no one can work. 5 While I am in the world, I am the light of the world."

6 Having said this, he spit on the ground, made some mud with the saliva, and put it on the man's eyes. 7 "Go" he told him, "wash in the Pool of Siloam" (this word means Sent). So the man went and washed, and came home seeing.

8 His neighbors and those who had formerly seen him begging asked, "Isn't this the same man who used to sit and beg?" 9 Some claimed that he was. Others said, "No, he only looks like him." But he himself insisted, "I am the man."

10 "How then were your eyes opened?" they demanded.

11 He replied, "The man they call Jesus made some mud and put it on my eyes. He told me to go to Siloam and wash. So I went and washed, and then I could see."

12 "Where is this man?" they asked him. "I don't know," he said.

13 They brought to the Pharisees the man who had been blind. 14 Now the day on which Jesus had made the mud and opened the man's eyes was a Sabbath. 15 Therefore the Pharisees also asked him how he had received his sight. "He put mud on my eyes," the man replied, "and I washed, and now I see."

16 Some of the Pharisees said, "This man is not from God, for he does not keep the Sabbath."

But others asked, "How can a sinner do such miraculous signs?" So they were divided.

17 Finally they turned again to the blind man, "What have you to say about him? It was your eyes he opened." The man replied, "He is a prophet."

18 The Jews still did not believe that he had been blind and had received his sight until they sent for the man's parents. 19 "Is this your son?" they asked. "Is this the one you say was born blind? How is it that now he can see?" 20 "We know he is our son," the parents answered, "and we know he was born blind. 21 But how he can see now, or who opened his eyes, we don't know. Ask him. He is of age; he will speak for himself." 22 His parents said this because they were afraid of the Jews, for already the Jews had decided that anyone who acknowledged that Jesus was the Christ would be put out of the synagogue. 23 That was why his parents said, "He is of age; ask him."

24 A second time they summoned the man who had been blind. "Give glory to God by telling the truth," they said, "We know this man is a sinner."

25 He replied, "Whether he is a sinner or not, I don't know. One thing I do know. I was blind and now I see!"

26 Then they asked him, "What did he do to you? How did he open your eyes?"

27 He answered, "I have told you already and you did not listen. Why do you want to hear it again? Do you want to become his disciples too?"

28 Then they hurled insults at him and said, "You are this fellow's disciple! We are disciples of Moses! 29 We know that God spoke to Moses, but as for this fellow, we don't know where he comes from."

30 The man answered, "Now that is remarkable! You don't know where he comes from, yet he opened my eyes. 31 We know that God does not listen to sinners. He listens to the godly man who does his will. 32 Nobody has ever heard of opening the eyes of a man born blind. 33 If this man were not from God, he could do nothing."

34 To this they replied, "You were steeped in sin at birth, how dare you lecture us!" And they threw him out.

35 Jesus heard that they had thrown him out, and when he found him, he said, "Do you believe in the Son of Man?"

36 "Who is he sir?" the man asked. "Tell me so that I may believe in him."

37 Jesus said, "You have now seen him; in fact, he is the one speaking with you."

38 Then the man said, "Lord, I believe," and he worshiped him.

REFLECTION

This healing account is dripping with interesting dialogue, irony, double meanings, assumptions, judgments, divisions, and new insight. It is more than a simple cure. It has all the drama of a well-written play yet it expresses some profound truths about Jesus and the ones who follow him. We have to sit back, take in all that it holds, and discover how it informs us about Jesus' mission to bring life and a new way of seeing. We can imagine being there to watch this drama unfold.

The first line of this account shows us the false assumptions within Jewish theology. They assumed that the man was born blind because of his sin or the parent's sin. They thought God was punishing these parents by making their son blind. Jesus dispels any idea that God would send disease or affliction as a punishment for a person's sins. We might punish ourselves by not taking care of ourselves, or others may punish us with their behavior, but God would never do that. *Abba* is perfect love and would not be *Abba* if he did anything other than be loving. Evil and human sinfulness, in general, cause disruption and illness in the world, but Jesus' miracles throughout the gospels demonstrated that he is on the side of wellness. Jesus helps us take back what we humans lost in paradise.

The healing itself is much like others we have seen. Jesus makes mud, puts it on the man's eyes, and tells him to go and wash. The word for putting the mud on the man's eyes carries the meaning that Jesus anointed the man's eyes with mud. We sometimes use blessed oil to do the same. The word to wash in this story is *baptize*. This story contains the double meaning that this man was not only cured but also baptized and became a disciple. He had life because he listened to Jesus, obeyed Jesus' direction, and now could "see" what life was really about.

The ensuing dialogue makes a whole play on who sees and who is blind. The Pharisees say that they know this man, Jesus, is a sinner. They assume that, but they do not know it. How often have you heard someone say they know something when, in fact, they do not know? The Pharisees are blinded by what they think is knowledge, and so they cannot see who Jesus is, nor can they see the miracle. Remember, earlier in this gospel, we read that the way to get to know Jesus is to "come and see," to let behind the old life and walk with him. This is the same today. Many do not see who Jesus is but judge him based on assumptions or what they think they know. They don't see the many miracles done in Jesus' name. They stay stuck in their old beliefs.

The apostle Paul wrote, *"Do not conform yourselves to this age but be transformed by the renewal of your mind, so that you may judge what is God's will, what is good, pleasing and perfect"* (Romans 12:2). Part of Jesus' healing ministry is giving new insight to our minds, to change our worldview, to see as he sees. We get it by listening to him and obeying like the blind man did. As healing ministers, we must let Jesus renew our minds and open us to the power of divine love. We must read and study the gospels to understand the compassionate heart of Jesus and his desire to have us feel the deep love that *Abba* has for us. We must see ourselves as Jesus sees us and others as he sees them. Then we can love as he loved.

It is an interesting dialogue between the neighbors who cannot figure out if this man is the one who was once blind or if he looks like him. They thought they knew him, but after he was "baptized," he looked different. Have you ever known someone who made a life-changing commitment to Jesus? They act differently and may even look differently. I have led many people to such a commitment, and their family often said they were a changed person. We feel and look different when we respond to Jesus' transforming love with a decision to follow him. We have new life.

This healing account not only describes the curing of a blind man's eyes but also demonstrates the richness of making a faith commitment to Jesus. This man is cured of his physical condition, and he is healed emotionally from years of false assumptions about himself. It must have been difficult to be judged as a sinner his whole life. He had done nothing wrong. Jesus' affirmation of his goodness and Jesus' cleansing love cause this man to make a full commitment to him. He went from feeling like a sinner to feeling like a son. The man saw life differently now and gave up his past in order to walk in the Light. There was a sacrifice he endured because of his new faith. The religious leaders badgered him for his newfound faith, but he was not going to let go of the one relationship that gave him life. They could insult and reject him but none of that mattered because now he had real life. If you imagine how this man was accused all his life, do you think anyone could have pulled him away from a relationship with a man who affirmed him and gave him new sight? He was not going to let go of Jesus. He was thrown out of his church community but discovered a much more life-giving community in the Trinity. He was healed physically, emotionally, and spiritually.

We can draw courage from this account when we are ridiculed for praying with people because of our faith. Once our eyes are opened to the healing power of Jesus' love in our lives and the lives of others, we cannot help but continue to offer that perfect love to others in his name. Only in him can we clearly see the purpose of our lives and live in true Peace. Once we see and feel the Peace, we want to stay with Jesus forever.

This account reminds us that God does not withhold favor from someone who has sinned. We all would be without favor if that were true. Jesus does not accuse but speaks truth and invites us to fashion our lives according to his words. He does not shame us but affirms us and heals the voices that hold us down and keep us from a full life. He wants us to have the fullness of life and live in his presence every day. This healing story offers a rich understanding of the heart of Jesus and the true purpose of his healing ministry. It ends with the final healing when the once blind man sees and worships Jesus. No one would ever take that away from him.

QUESTIONS TO PONDER/DISCUSS

- What do you think it was like to be the blind man? What was it like after he met Jesus?
- Do you know people who do not believe that Jesus is the Son of God? What do you say?
- Can you think of a time when you may have gotten shunned or pushed out of your church for offering healing prayers to others?
- What can we learn about blindness and healing from this account?

PRACTICAL APPLICATION

Share with someone who Jesus is for you and how you came to know him.

HEALING ACCOUNT 22

Blind, Dumb, and Possessed Man

READ MATTHEW 12:22-28 (THIS ACCOUNT IS ALSO FOUND IN MARK 20-27 AND LUKE 11:14-26)

22 Then they brought him a demon-possessed man who was blind and mute, and Jesus healed him, so that he could both talk and see. 23 All the people were astonished and said, "Could this be the Son of David?"

24 But when the Pharisees heard this, they said, "It is only by Beelzebub, the prince of demons, that this fellow drives out demons."

25 Jesus knew their thoughts and said to them, "Every kingdom divided against itself will be ruined, and every city or household divided against itself will not stand. 26 If Satan drives out Satan, he is divided against himself. How then can his kingdom stand? 27 And if I drive out demons by Beelzebub, by whom do your people drive them out? So then, they will be your judges. 28 But if I drive out demons by the Spirit of God, then the kingdom of God has come upon you."

READ MARK 3:20-27

20 Then Jesus entered a house, and again a crowd gathered, so that his disciples were not even able to eat. 21

When his family heard about this, they went to take charge of him, for they said, "He is out of his mind."
22 And the teachers of the law who came down from Jerusalem said, "He is possessed by Beelzebub! By the prince of demons, he is driving out demons."

REFLECTION

Some interesting dialogue accompanies this healing account. Matthew's account tells the miracle, and Mark's account adds some additional issues related to this healing. Both accounts address the same situation and the people's response.

The miracle itself is told in a very short manner. It is straightforward. The people's reaction shows their astonishment and anticipation of the coming of the Son of David or the Messiah. This healing gave them hope that they might see that day of freedom. They realized they may be standing in his presence. When we witness a healing, it is awesome to think that we are right in the presence where Jesus showed up. Many from our healing teams through the years were overwhelmed to stand in the healing presence of Jesus. One time, after a healing day in our church on Saturday, a man walked into church on Sunday morning and said, "What went on in here? I can feel an energy that I never felt before." He was not connected to the healing ministry in any way, but he picked up the divine presence that had filled that place the day before and was still there. Some people would walk into our church and begin to cry because they felt the love of God so deeply there.

Interestingly, as in many others, this account shows that the people were astonished while the leaders tried to stop it. In many cases, the response to the healing ministry of Jesus is the same today. Often, lay people can appreciate the beauty of a miracle, but the leaders get caught in the web of their theological training, which causes them to question the gift. Many leaders are told that these things never happened, so they struggle to appreciate a miracle when it occurs. I broke out of that web when I came to know Jesus in a deeper way and saw his healing power move in my midst.

Blind, Dumb, and Possessed Man

Mark's account of the aftermath of this healing and deliverance tells of Jesus' family, who seem to be concerned for him. They had a reason for their concern. The religious authorities were getting very angry because Jesus disregarded some of the 613 laws in their tradition. Jesus was more concerned about relieving people's pain and setting them free than following those minor laws. His compassionate heart compelled him to offer healing when someone was in pain. I recall one time when I said I was going to celebrate a healing Eucharist with prayer for healing. A liturgist told me I was not allowed to do that because praying with people for healing during a communion service was not liturgically correct. I felt sad that she did not understand the healing power of the Eucharist and how it puts people in an atmosphere to receive healing. I celebrated many such healing Eucharists and watched thousands of people get well. Others were angry because I did not follow all the liturgical "rules." Some little rules are not as important as offering God's people an atmosphere of healing and hope.

It is an interesting statement that the family made. They said he was "out of his mind." We may not know what they meant, but we can reflect on the deeper meaning of those words. I believe Jesus was out of his mind because he put on the mind of *Abba*. He was directed from above. He was not teaching like his peers because he was listening to a different voice. If we allow ourselves to be "transformed by the renewal of our mind," one could say that we are also out of our mind. We start thinking like Jesus and following his direction. We might live differently than people around us, taking time for daily prayer, worshiping every Sunday, reading the Bible, and praying for the healing of people. That is what scripture calls being in our "right mind." That is living the fullness of life, even if some people do not understand. Those who are looking for greater peace and joy in their life will be influenced in a good way by us. We must offer an alternative to just worldly thinking. That is what Jesus did.

Mark's account mentioned that the crowd was so large that the disciples were unable to eat. Once in a while, the healing ministry can be overwhelming, and people keep coming and wanting more. People want to receive the anointing of Jesus' love. If we are part of this ministry, there can be some sacrifices for us to be available for others, but we must also practice self-care. If we do not take care of ourselves, we will not be good for anyone. There is a time to pull away and rest as needed. The disciples would eventually do this, and so must we.

The Pharisees and religious leaders could not figure out how Jesus had power over evil. Since they did not accept Jesus as the Son of God, they could not understand his source of power. To them, he was an ordinary man. Since they did not seek the real power source, they assumed he got his power from Beelzebub, the prince of demons. Jesus challenges their logic by asking, "How can Satan drive out Satan?" He points out that a kingdom divided against itself cannot stand. Today, some people will not acknowledge the power of Jesus to heal, and they attribute miracles to some lesser force. Like Jesus, we have to debunk their skewed thinking and affirm the power of Jesus' presence in the world today. In his book, *Love Your God with All Your Mind*, J. P. Moreland gives excellent examples of how to respond to the illogical arguments people make about spiritual and moral issues. We must begin by acknowledging that Jesus is the Son of God and then accept his ministry and teachings as divine.

Jesus says that to enter a strong man's house, a person has to be able to tie up the strong man. He is the only one who could bind Satan and cast him out of a person. We have seen before that if we are going to participate in deliverance ministry, we must be very closely connected to Jesus and only operate in the power of his name. Then, we can invade and take over Satan's area and displace him from a person into the hands of Jesus. Once we have displaced Satan, we pray for healing of the area where he had resided.

BLIND, DUMB, AND POSSESSED MAN

QUESTIONS TO PONDER/DISCUSS

- How do you think this man changed after he could talk and see?
- Who are all the people in this account who needed healing?
- Can you distinguish how thinking like Jesus differs from thinking like the culture?
- What can we glean from this account?

PRACTICAL APPLICATION

Break into groups of two. One person prays for the other while the other receives. Pray that the person will receive words to say when seeking to witness about Jesus. Pray that they will see each person they meet with the eyes of Jesus. Then switch roles.

HEALING ACCOUNT 23

A Crippled Woman

READ LUKE 13:10-17

10 On a Sabbath Jesus was teaching in one of the synagogues, and a woman was there who had been crippled by a spirit for eighteen years. She was bent over and could not straighten up at all. 12 When Jesus saw her, he called her forward and said to her, "Woman, you are set free from your infirmity." 13 Then he put his hands on her, and immediately she straightened up and praised God.

14 Indignant because Jesus had healed on the Sabbath, the synagogue ruler said to the people, "There are six days for work. So come and be healed on those days, not on the Sabbath."

15 The Lord answered him, "You hypocrites! Doesn't each of you on the Sabbath untie his ox or donkey from the stall and lead it out to give it water? 16 Then should not this woman, a daughter of Abraham, whom Satan has kept bound for eighteen long years, be set free on the Sabbath day from what bound her?"

17 When he said this, all his opponents were humiliated, but the people were delighted with all the wonderful things he was doing.

A Crippled Woman

REFLECTION

We can imagine how this woman felt after living eighteen years in a crippled state. The account indicates that she was desperate since she came into the synagogue. Jesus called her forward, told her she was free from the infirmity, and laid his hands on her. Immediately, she straightened up. Being in Jesus' presence brought about amazing results.

Again, we read how the synagogue ruler was indignant because Jesus broke one of the little Sabbath rules. However, Jesus responded by pointing out that the religious leaders also break their Sabbath rule by leading their donkey or ox to water on the Sabbath. They did not want Jesus to break their human-made rules but felt comfortable breaking them themselves. They were keeping people in the prison of their infirmity with these rules, while they did as they pleased. The people's reaction to Jesus' healing of the woman showed that they did not believe in all the little human rules. They were delighted that Jesus was setting people free.

This account reminds me of a time when we were in Eindhoven in the Netherlands. We celebrated a large healing Eucharist and then commissioned the prayer ministers there to pray with the 800 people in the church. We had to leave, but the prayer ministry went on for a long time. The next morning, we read about that service in the paper and how a woman who had been bent over for many years was healed and stood up straight. God had empowered an amazing healing. It was good to see a story like that make the city paper. What I also found refreshing was that the woman was healed when we, as leaders were no longer there. It happened through the prayer ministers. People sometimes think that healing can only happen through priests or famous people but in fact every Christian has the power to offer Jesus' healing love through their deep connection to Jesus. The more that Christians are connected to him in prayer and open to the gifts of the Holy Spirit, the more energy of his love can flow through them and change lives.

This account also invites us to think about where we or others are "bent over" in pain. What kind of wounds bend us over in pain or cripple us? It may be years of unresolved grief. It may be fear that cripples us emotionally. It may be living with an unforgiven sin that alienates us from others. It may be unforgiveness that we harbor in our heart which causes anger and resentment. Jesus invites us to be set free through the power of his forgiving and healing love. He offers us this gift because he does not want to see us live in pain. He offers us this gift so that we can "stand up straight" and offer the same gift to others. No power on earth can stop us.

Once we accept Jesus' freeing love, we are more prepared to set others free in his name. We start by listening to people and allowing them to share their pain. This takes an intentional person-centered listening. It means putting aside other distractions and letting the person know that we hear them. Thirty percent of healing happens during this time of listening to someone. We can understand them if we have made the journey to wellness or at least are on the journey. We can have empathy because someone first had empathy for us. This kind of listening is a treasure that we have to offer.

My friend told the story of how he prayed with a woman who had been estranged from her daughter. She had arthritis in her knees. He prayed for both her and her daughter. She forgave her daughter. The woman said that her spirit had been set free. Her knees were healed, and her relationship with her daughter was mended. Jesus' healing ministry continues today through people who draw life and energy from God.

Jesus' response to the synagogue ruler is that this woman had been bound for eighteen years. It was time to set her free. We might reflect on how many people are bound by fear, shame, legalism, or a need to control. Jesus wants to set them free. We are commissioned to offer them true freedom found in Jesus. Through our listening, our compassionate heart, and our healing prayers we can invite them to be free in Jesus' name.

A CRIPPLED WOMAN

QUESTIONS TO PONDER/DISCUSS

- Where do you see people bent over in pain?
- What gifts do you feel you have to set people free and experience healing?
- Do you have a place where you can pray with people for healing?
- What can we take away from this account?

PRACTICAL APPLICATION

Break into groups of two. Take some time to consider your deepest pain. If you wish to share it with your prayer partner, do so, and then have them pray for healing of that deep pain. They can also pray for it without you sharing what it is. Then exchange roles. You may also think of people you know who are in great pain. Take time to pray for them.

HEALING ACCOUNT 24

The Man with Dropsy

READ LUKE 14:1-6

1 One Sabbath when Jesus went to eat in the house of a prominent Pharisee, he was being carefully watched. 2 There in front of him was a man suffering from dropsy. 3 Jesus asked the Pharisees and experts in the law, "Is it lawful to heal on the Sabbath or not?" 4 But they remained silent. So taking hold of the man, he healed him and sent him away.

5 Then he asked them, "If one of you has a son or an ox that falls into a well on the Sabbath day, will you not immediately pull him out?" 6 And they had nothing to say.

REFLECTION

There is a unique comment in this healing account. It says Jesus *"was being carefully watched."* It is ironic because if the leaders had carefully watched Jesus go off to pray, and show divine compassion, and care for people as he did, they would have believed in him. They would have been able to see who he was if they were carefully watching. They watched but did not see because they did not want to submit to his message. They only watched to see if he would do something wrong rather than watching for the wonderful things he was doing to bring life and wholeness to people. Many people know who Jesus is and even read the Bible, but they do not want to accept his message and surrender to his will. They look for some way to find fault with him so they can disregard his teachings. They deny that he is the Son of God so that they do not have to accept his instruction and change their ways.

As Christians, people sometimes carefully watch us to see if we will mess up or do something out of line. Belonging to Jesus carries a responsibility to live as he taught. Our life witness is important in bringing more people to the freedom and wholeness that Jesus desires for them. If we do mess up, it is imperative that we repent and get back on the road to life. A Jesus-led life witness is the greatest tool for bringing more people to a relationship with Jesus. We spread the gospel by living the gospel. We have a chance to evangelize without saying a word.

Dropsy is a disease in which fluid accumulates beneath the skin and causes swelling and pain. Again, we see Jesus respond to this person's pain with his healing touch. If he were going to be watched, he would do what would be life-giving for this hurting man. He did it immediately without waiting for the Pharisees' response. I learned that there is no better time to pray with a person than right when they ask for it. We might have to follow up later, but the request opens the door for healing love to flow.

This account invites us to reflect on what things get under our skin and cause pain. It may not be fluid, but some irritations can send us off in hurt or anger. We might ask ourselves, "What people get under my skin and cause pain? What is unresolved in me that they can irritate and inflame?" Jesus came to cure physical conditions and to heal the root causes, which may include traumatic events, bitter root judgments, or inner vows from early childhood. We are invited to look within and consider what issues in our lives are unresolved and cause us pain. We can invite Jesus back through our memories, experiences, and choices. We can let his love soak out any discord and feel his awesome love setting us free. Once we are healed of our inner wounds, people can no longer irritate us in those areas.

As we experience Jesus' setting us free, we are better able to see other people's pain beneath their irritating words or actions. This gives us a chance to begin praying for them and takes the focus off what they may have said or done. Sometimes, just taking in a couple big breaths of Jesus' love allows us to feel a deep peace so that we do not get irritated by their words or actions. We can live in the protection of Jesus' love and be sustained by his divine peace. From this vantage point, we can help others be freed of the things that get under their skin.

We have seen that Jesus often healed on the Sabbath. The Sabbath was meant to be a day of freedom, a holy day of resting and restoring life. Jesus was trying to model this original understanding. The Sabbath had become a day of restrictions. People could not cook, walk too far, carry any load, or heal another person. Jesus tried to break through those restrictive laws and invite people to celebrate the life-giving power of God's love. It is a day to worship God and enjoy resting in the divine presence. We can be part of restoring this original meaning of the Sabbath.

QUESTIONS TO PONDER/DISCUSS

- What are your thoughts about being watched as a Christian?
- Who needed healing in this account?
- How do you celebrate the Sabbath/Sunday? Is it life-giving?
- What can we learn from this account?

PRACTICAL APPLICATION

A powerful time to experience healing is after receiving Communion. Be attentive to Jesus within you after receiving Communion. See if you can work out a way to pray with someone after your Sunday Communion service.

HEALING ACCOUNT 25

Ten Lepers

READ LUKE 17:11-19

11 Now on his way to Jerusalem, Jesus traveled along the border between Samaria and Galilee. 12 As he was going into a village, ten men who had leprosy met him. They stood at a distance 13 and called out in a loud voice, "Jesus, Master, have pity on us!"

14 When he saw them, he said, "Go, show yourselves to the priests." And as they went they were cleansed.

15 One of them, when he saw he was healed, came back, praising God in a loud voice. 16 He threw himself at Jesus' feet and thanked him—and he was a Samaritan.

17 Jesus asked him, "Were not all ten cleansed? Where are the other nine? 18 Was no one found to return and give praise to God except this foreigner?" 19 Then he said to him, "Rise and go; your faith has made you well."

REFLECTION

In this account, we again read of Jesus' power to heal at a distance. The lepers were required to keep a distance from everyone. In this story, they shout out to Jesus for help. Their request indicates their belief in Jesus' power to cure them. When they followed Jesus' instruction and went off to show themselves to the priests, they were cleansed. Jesus cured their skin disease, and then they had to decide how to respond to the gift. Jesus responded to their felt need, hoping they might be healed of their deeper need.

The account says that one of them, seeing that he was cured, came back to Jesus, praising God. He threw himself at Jesus' feet and thanked him. Giving praise and thanks to God is an important part of the healing ministry. It keeps our focus on the true life-giver and off ourselves. This man took the occasion of the cure to enter into a relationship with Jesus. Jesus said to him, *"Your faith has made you well."* The word *well* changes. It says all ten were cured (*iathe*), but the one who came back and connected to Jesus in faith was made well (*sesoken*). His return and commitment to Jesus gave him the greater healing. He would live forever.

The gospels do not say that people needed faith to be cured. If they wanted to be well forever, they needed to enter a faith relationship with Jesus as this one man did. Jesus could cure all ten because of his deep healing love, but he could only make one man well. He needed the response of faith and surrender to offer the man true wellness and fullness of life. As ministers of healing, we need to have a deep faith relationship with Jesus and bring his divine healing love to people in need. His love is what cures. Being baptized in the Holy Spirit fills us with that extravagant, divine love and the gifts of the Holy Spirit to minister it. We bathe people in the healing love of Jesus, and if they respond with a desire to be connected to Jesus, we can invite them to enter a life-saving relationship with Jesus. If they accept, they can be well forever.

This account indicates Jesus' readiness to heal a Samaritan. As we saw in the healing of the woman at the well, Jesus stepped through the cultural Jewish ban on talking with Samaritans and offered healing. Samaritans were considered outcasts not because of what they did but because of their ancestors. They had intermarried with non-Jews centuries earlier. Jesus made no judgment against Samaritans. The man he made well experienced physical and spiritual healing and probably emotional healing after being welcomed by a Jew. Jesus' healing love touches all dimensions of a person's life. As healing ministers, we are challenged to put aside any judgments about certain people and offer Jesus' healing love to all.

If we do not have love for a person, we may need to examine our hearts and, if necessary, repent of our judgment. We might pray for the love of God to transform our human love so that we can offer the full power of God's love to the person in need. We can be honest about our humanness but must be receptive to the divine power to transform us into an instrument of Jesus' healing love.

We can offer a certain power for healing to people at a distance. We can bathe a person in Jesus' healing love through a phone call or just our intercessory prayer. A study was done where a group prayed for people with rheumatoid arthritis. The study showed that the people who received in-person prayer and laying on of hands made greater improvement than those who received prayer at a distance. We are called to do both, but if we can pray in person, it seems to be more effective. What is important is that we listen to what God asks of us in that situation.

QUESTIONS TO PONDER/DISCUSS

- What was Jesus doing at the time of this miracle? Why do you think he stopped?
- Where do you think that man who came back to Jesus ended up?
- How do you overcome judgments against certain people?
- What can we learn from this account?

PRACTICAL APPLICATION

Take time to tell someone that you will pray for them for a certain time. Ask them if they experienced any relief or a deeper sense of peace at the end of that time.

HEALING ACCOUNT 26

Zacchaeus

READ LUKE 19:1-10

1 Jesus entered Jericho and was passing through. 2 A man was there by the name of Zacchaeus; he was a chief tax collector and was wealthy. 3 He wanted to see who Jesus was, but being a short man, he could not, because of the crowd. 4 So he ran ahead and climbed a sycamore-fig tree to see him, since Jesus was coming that way.

5 When Jesus reached the spot, he looked up and said to him, "Zacchaeus, come down immediately, I mean to stay at your house today." 6 So he came down at once and welcomed him gladly.

7 All the people saw this and began to mutter, "He has gone to be the guest of a 'sinner.'"

8 But Zacchaeus stood up and said to the Lord, "Look, Lord! Here and now I give half of my possessions to the poor, and if I have cheated anybody out of anything, I will pay back four times the amount."

9 Jesus said to him, "Today salvation has come to this house, because this man, too, is a son of Abraham. 10 For the Son of Man came to seek and to save the lost."

Zacchaeus

REFLECTION

I am adding this account because it speaks so much about bringing healing and salvation to someone who is entangled in destructive practices. It is about the transforming love of Jesus. I believe Zacchaeus wanted to see Jesus because although he was rich, he was lonely, living outside the Jewish community. He was collecting taxes for the occupying government, and as such, he was hurting his brother and sister Jews. In addition to that, as a tax collector, he took extra money for his own pocket. That is why the people mutter about Jesus' decision to go to his house.

Stop and consider what other responses Jesus could have made to Zacchaeus when he came to the place under the tree. He could have chided him for what he was doing to his fellow Jews. Jesus could have walked by because Zacchaeus was outside of the Jewish community. He could have judged him and told him to straighten out his life. Instead, he shows him divine love by inviting him down from the tree and welcoming him. Zacchaeus was caught in his lifestyle and no one else gave him a way to get out of it except Jesus.

There was a price to accept Jesus' invitation, but the pain of being up a tree in loneliness and the pain of separation must have been greater than the money he would give away. Jesus' love for him gave him the strength to make a life change, to turn around, and to begin living in peace and right relationship with Jesus and the community. This is a powerful story about the power of Jesus' love to transform lives. Loving people with his love brings healing as we have seen in the previous healing stories, but it also creates an environment for a radical change of heart. It gave Zacchaeus the desire to make things right. Jesus accepted everyone, and then his presence called everyone to repent and align their life practices with his teachings. It is part of our healing mission. If we love people with the love of Jesus, we give them the space and the energy to break out of the entanglements of certain destructive practices.

Zacchaeus was a wounded man. Why would he turn on his fellow Jews and steal from them? He must have had some hurtful experiences that caused him to live as he did, alienated from his community. Maybe, since he was short, he was bullied as a child or called names. We do not know the story, but we know that Jesus' acceptance gave him a way to change his behavior and be at peace. Zacchaeus had to decide to accept this invitation. Jesus saw beneath Zacchaeus' practices and ministered to the hurting little man, and that little man had been waiting for someone to notice his wounded heart. He ministers to the child within each person to bring them the fullness of life. He also ministers to the child within us to bring us healing, and his ministry challenges us to do the same. His healing ministry went to the core issues, which, when healed, caused people to change and live in a relationship with him.

Even though Jesus invited Zacchaeus to come down and told him he meant to stay at his house, he did not condone his destructive behavior. Jesus taught that certain practices were destructive to humans and human relationships. Some of those are recorded in Mark 7:22–23. He did not want people to live with destructive behaviors in their lives. He wanted people to experience the deep joy and peace of living as the Creator intended. He invited Zacchaeus into that life. As in the physical healings we explored, Jesus' mission was to make people well and live in an eternal relationship with him. Each one who wanted real life had to change what was not in keeping with Jesus' teaching and enter into a faith relationship with him. Zacchaeus does that, and so he has life; he has salvation.

Many people live alienated and in pain. Some carry a deep father or mother wound within them; some feel a deep shame, have very low self-esteem, or carry a heavy load of unresolved grief. All of these can cause people to act out in destructive ways and get entangled in destructive relationships. They may be waiting for someone to see the wounded person beneath their behavior. When we welcome these people and let them know that we see their pain, we allow them to share the pain and change their destructive behavior. They do not always choose healing and serenity, but our part is to make the offer. If we allow Jesus to heal our deep hurts and change our behavior, we can hear and respond to others in the same way.

There are other people who are not caught up in destructive behavior but live with inner pains. They seem to be living all right, but they silently suffer on the inside. A song called "Friend of a Wounded Heart" made me more aware of this group. This song speaks of people who say they are fine and try to keep a smile, but underneath, there is some deep pain. They hide their empty longing for love and try to keep their heart concealed. In reality, they want someone to see and acknowledge that they see their pain. They want a place to release their pain and feel genuine love. Creating an atmosphere for this to happen is part of the healing ministry.

As ministers of healing, we are challenged to see beneath the façade that some people present and minister to the heart of the person. Being attentive to what people say and listening with the heart of Jesus gives us a chance to hear their aching hearts and dry the tears that no one sees. They can be set free with Jesus' healing love and our gentle care. I have seen so many people transform when someone responds to the pain within with the accepting love of Jesus. Jesus, in this story of Zacchaeus, models for us how to do that and gives us a chance to get free if we carry inner pain. He desires to "stay in our house" and lavish his deep love on us every day.

QUESTIONS TO PONDER/DISCUSS

- If you were in the crowd, how would you have reacted when Jesus welcomed Zacchaeus down from the tree?
- Why do you think Zacchaeus was willing to give up so much of his money?
- Have you ever ministered to the inner pain that someone was silently carrying?
- What can we take away from this account?

Experience the Healing Miracles of Jesus

PRACTICAL APPLICATION

Listen for who may be carrying pain on the inside. Ask God to give you the words that would give them a chance to share their pain. Take time to be available for a healing conversation.

HEALING ACCOUNT 27

The Raising of Lazarus

READ JOHN 11:1-46

1 Now a man named Lazarus was sick. He was from Bethany, the village of Mary and her sister Martha. 2 Mary, whose brother Lazarus now lay sick, was the same one who poured perfume on the Lord and wiped his feet with her hair. 3 The sisters sent word to Jesus, "Lord, the one you love is sick."

4 When he heard this, Jesus said, "This sickness will not end in death. No, it is for God's glory so that God's Son may be glorified through it."

5 Jesus loved Martha and her sister and Lazarus. 6 Yet when he heard that Lazarus was sick, he stayed where he was two more days. 7 Then he said to his disciples, "Let us go back to Judea."

8 "But Rabbi," they said, "a short while ago the Jews tried to stone you, and yet you are going back there?"

9 Jesus answered, "Are there not twelve hours of daylight? A man who walks by day will not stumble, for he sees by this world's light. 10 It is when he walks by night that he stumbles, for he has no light."

11 After he had said this, he went on to tell them, "Our friend Lazarus has fallen asleep; but I am going there to wake him up."

12 His disciples replied, "Lord, if he sleeps, he will get better."

13 Jesus had been speaking of his death, but his disciples thought he meant natural sleep. 14 So then he told them plainly, "Lazarus is dead, 15 and for your sake I am glad I was not there, so that you may believe. But let us go to him."

16 Then Thomas said to the rest of the disciples, "Let us also go, that we may die with him."

17 On his arrival, Jesus found that Lazarus had already been in the tomb for four days. 18 Bethany was less than two miles from Jerusalem, 19 and many Jews had come to Martha and Mary to comfort them in the loss of their brother. 20 When Martha heard that Jesus was coming, she went out to meet him, but Mary stayed at home.21. "Lord," Martha said to Jesus, "if you had been here, my brother would not have died. 22 But I know that even now God will give you whatever you ask."

23 Jesus said to her, "Your brother will rise again."

24 Martha answered, "I know he will rise again in the resurrection at the last day."

25 Jesus said to her, "I am the resurrection and the life. He who believes in me will live, even though he dies, 26 and whoever lives and believes in me will never die. Do you believe this?"

27 "Yes, Lord," she told him, "I believe that you are the Christ, the Son of God, who was to come into the world."

28 And after she had said this, she went back and called her sister Mary aside, "The teacher is here," she said, "and is asking for you." 29 When Mary heard this, she got up quickly and went to him. 30 Now Jesus had not yet entered the village, but was still at the place where Martha had met him. 31 When the Jews who had been with Mary in the house, comforting her, noticed how quickly she got up and went out, they followed her, supposing she was going to the tomb to mourn there.

32 When Mary reached the place where Jesus was and saw him, she fell at his feet and said, "Lord, if you had been here, my brother would not have died."

33 When Jesus saw her weeping, and the Jews who had come along with her also weeping, he was deeply moved in spirit and troubled. 34 "Where have you laid him?" he asked.

THE RAISING OF LAZARUS

"Come and see, Lord," they replied.
35 Jesus wept.
36 Then the Jews said, "See how he loved him!"
37 But some of them said, "Could not he who opened the eyes of the blind man have kept this man from dying?"
38 Jesus, once more deeply moved, came to the tomb. It was a cave with a stone laid across the entrance. 39 "Take away the stone," he said.
"But, Lord," said Martha, the sister of the dead man, "by this time there is a bad odor, for he has been there four days."
40 Then Jesus said, "Did I not tell you that if you believed, you would see the glory of God?"
41 So they took away the stone. Then Jesus looked up and said, "Father, I thank you that you have heard me.
42 I knew that you always hear me, but I said this for the benefit of the people standing here, that they may believe that you sent me."
43 When he had said this, Jesus called out in a loud voice, "Lazarus, come out!"
44 The dead man came out, his hands and feet wrapped with strips of linen, and a cloth around his face. Jesus said to them, "Take off the grave clothes and let him go."
45 Therefore many of the Jews who had come to visit Mary, and had seen what Jesus did, put their faith in him.
46 But some of them went to the Pharisees and told them what Jesus had done.

REFLECTION

We have read a number of accounts where Jesus raised a person from the dead. Each of these accounts takes us to a new level of understanding as to who Jesus is. He carried the creative love of *Abba* so intensely that he could re-create a life. Even though we may never have seen this happen, the fact that he did it gives us a new view of life. Death is not the final word when we are connected to Jesus and live in the presence of his love. This story has many facets and offers some important examples of ministering in situations where death has occurred. We put ourselves at the scene and watch this divine ministry unfold.

At the beginning of this account, we read that Lazarus, Martha, and Mary were friends of Jesus. Jesus loved everyone with divine love, but he also had friendships as we do. He probably stopped at their house when he traveled to Jerusalem. It is good to know that Jesus had friends. Here, he ministers to some of his dear friends.

As we reflect on this story, we might ask ourselves who is in need? Lazarus had an obvious need, but his sisters also had a need. The disciples had a need if, we consider their fear of Jesus going close to Jerusalem, where he had almost been stoned to death. It is interesting to watch how Jesus ministers to each of their needs.

First, Jesus addressed the disciples' fear by telling them they must walk in the light. If they stay within the Father's will, they will be safe. We notice the irony in Thomas' statement, "Let us go, that we may die with him." They had to be committed to Jesus, ready to die with him, to have real life. Once they were ready to die, then they were ready to live. Jesus would show them how he gives true and lasting life. Only when we are ready to die to ourselves and follow Jesus wherever he takes us can we truly live.

Then, Martha also had a need. At first, it was a fear that her brother might die. Later, it was the grief because her brother had died. Jesus did not respond to her first need because he felt the Father had a more important plan. He waited two days after hearing of Lazarus' illness. Jesus operated in the Divine timeline to bring a key message to the world. When he came to Bethany he ministered to Martha's grief first. He offered words of comfort. He said, "Your brother will rise again." These words of comfort still bring comfort and hope to people today. Through our belief in this statement, we can bring healing and hope to people who have lost loved ones. We can stand with people in their loss, offering them resurrection hope. Martha expressed her belief that Jesus could bring new life to her brother. She found comfort in those words.

Jesus made a profound statement at this point that changed the way we view human life. He said, *"I am the resurrection and the* life. *The one who believes in me will live, even if he dies, and whoever lives and believes in me will never die."* Again, the word for life here is Zoe. We saw it in the first account of the healing of the royal official's son. It means a life connected to Jesus, a life that is filled with great peace and serenity and is eternal. This promise of Jesus gives believers a whole new worldview. It takes us beyond what we see to what Jesus sees for us. It empowered the first Christians and many after them to lay down their life in this world for the fullness of life in heaven. This message continues to give hope in times of loss. We can bring the resurrected presence of Jesus and the promise of new life to those in grief.

Next, Jesus ministered to Mary's need. After meeting her and seeing her grief, the scripture says, *"Jesus wept."* That short verse carries some profound healing ointment. His ministry was first to cry with her. He entered her pain and gave her permission to cry. He gave all of us permission to cry and let the tears wash the toxins out of our system. He revealed his human heart that hurt, a heart that was moved with compassion when he saw someone hurting. We can feel him standing with us in our pain, offering hope, and giving us, as healing ministers, a model for ministry. We realize that feeling someone else's pain is part of the sacrifice of the healing ministry. Sometimes, there are no words, just tears shared in love, but we do so with a message of hope and new life.

In our culture, there is a tendency to want to avoid tears and grieving, but releasing the pain with someone else is very important to our health. The celebration of a funeral right after the death of a loved one is the most healing thing we can do. Gathering, telling the stories, crying together, sharing healing embraces, and celebrating the promise of resurrection is cleansing and healing for the family and friends. There is a temptation to put off this process and have a celebration of life later, but by then, the grief has been stuffed down and often remains in our system. In this account, Jesus models a healthy way to grieve our losses, showing that he stands with us in our pain.

This account offers us a picture of how to grieve other losses in our lives. When we feel Jesus with us, we can have the courage to "take away the stones" we may have placed in front of some of the losses in our lives. Life has losses, and it is imperative that we grieve them, especially those losses that do not have a funeral. Lost dreams, loss of health, divorce, loss of friends when moving to a new area, loss of children who "go away." All of these losses can get buried in our hearts and "taking away the stone" with a friend and in the presence of Jesus can be very healing and bring about deep peace. As healing ministers, it is important to be attentive to people's repressed grief and offer them a chance to process their pain and feel Jesus with them.

A high percentage of addictive behavior comes from repressed unresolved grief. If people carry a huge amount of unresolved grief, they often seek to feel relief from the pain by medicating it with alcohol, drugs, food or other behaviors. It gives them temporary relief but afterwards it makes the pain even worse. It does not address the core issue. Jesus' healing love can be a significant part of helping them "taking away the stones" that are holding their grief within. My work in some recovery programs showed me how powerful it is for Jesus' love to help process and heal the repressed grief. It gives hope of new life and freedom where hope may have been lost.

Lastly, Jesus ministers to Lazarus. He gives us an image of his source of power when he looked up and said, "Father, I thank you that you have heard me." Through his love connection with the Father, he is able to raise the dead. This is the same love connection that raised him from the dead. He then called out to Lazarus to "come out." Lazarus responded to the call and walked out of the tomb. He had been freed from death's hold because he heard the voice of Jesus and followed it. If we only see a man walking out of the tomb, we miss the double miracle in this story. Lazarus knew Jesus, but now he heard the Good Shepherd call him and followed that voice. John 10:14–15 says the Good Shepherd knows his sheep and they know him. It is a life-giving knowledge, a life-giving relationship. Lazarus now knew the Shepherd more deeply. He now had life that would last forever. He was raised to life and chose a deeper connection to the Good Shepherd. Now, he had the fullness of life, and he would never die.

Then, the words spoken by Jesus earlier to Martha make more sense. He said, *"I am the resurrection and the life. The one who believes in me will live, even though he dies, and whoever lives and believes in me will never die."* This account gives us hope of eternal life. It is the promise of a connection that lasts forever. We see that in many of the healing stories, Jesus tries to invite people into this faith relationship so that they will live forever. The cures were an invitation to have life. If we participate in the healing ministry of Jesus, we can offer that same hope to those to whom we minister. Jesus' healing ministry was unique in this regard. He invites us to offer this unique gift to people in our life.

This account expands our worldview and allows us to "see" beyond this life. It puts all of life into a new perspective. If people are open to this vision, they can live life with much more peace, joy, and serenity. Jesus said, *"If you believed, you would see the glory of God."* We can see the glory of God every day when we live in the life Jesus offers.

QUESTIONS TO PONDER/DISCUSS

- What do you think it was like to be a friend of Jesus and have him stay at your house?
- How can we stay attentive to God's timing when we offer healing ministry?
- How have you helped people process their grief and their unresolved grief?
- What can we glean from this account?

PRACTICAL APPLICATION

Share with someone any grief that you hold inside. Listen to the grief they hold inside. Pray for Jesus' love to help you "take away the stones" you may have placed in front of those griefs to hold them in.

HEALING ACCOUNT 28

A Blind Beggar

READ MARK 10:46–52 (THIS ACCOUNT IS ALSO FOUND IN MATTHEW 20:29–34 AND LUKE 18:35–43)

46 Then they came to Jericho. As Jesus and his disciples, together with a large crowd, were leaving the city, a blind man, Bartimaeus (that is, the Son of Timaeus), was sitting by the roadside begging. 57 When he heard that it was Jesus of Nazareth, he began to shout, "Jesus, Son of David, have mercy on me!"

48 Many rebuked him and told him to be quiet, but he shouted all the more, "Son of David, have mercy on me!"

49 Jesus stopped and said, "Call him."

So they called to the blind man, "Cheer up! On your feet! He's calling you." 50 Throwing his cloak aside, he jumped to his feet and came to Jesus.

51 "What do you want me to do for you?" Jesus asked him. The blind man said, "Rabbi, I want to see."

52 "Go," said Jesus, "your faith has healed you." Immediately he received his sight and followed Jesus up the road.

REFLECTION

We have read several accounts where Jesus cured blindness. This one is somewhat unique in that it contains a deeper healing. This

A Blind Beggar

blind beggar calls out to Jesus. He calls him Son of David, a title for the Messiah. In his book *Mark, Good News for Hard Times*, George Montague points out that the beggar's use of the name *Jesus* is even more unusual. No one to this point had used Jesus' personal name when asking for a cure. This man felt a closeness to Jesus, and the story shows that he was ready to walk with him to Jerusalem. Jesus responded to his faith with the statement, "your faith has made you well. Here Jesus used the word for the deeper healing (*sesoken*). The curing of his sight prompted him to commit his life to Jesus and be well forever.

There are significant indications that this blind beggar was ready to commit to Jesus. When Jesus called him, he *"threw off his cloak."* That is not ordinary behavior for a blind man. Recall that garments in the gospels convey the disposition of a person, their personality. This man was ready to change his disposition and follow Jesus. We can also consider that his cloak was everything he had. That represented his whole life but he wanted to make a radical change. He believed he would get his sight and go from being alongside the road to being on the road with Jesus. He was ready to make a change in life. After he did get his sight, the account says he *"followed Jesus up the road."* He received not only a cure but wholeness, a transformed life. That is a profound statement. That road was going to Jerusalem where Jesus would be crucified.

This healing account, like many others, portrays the main reason Jesus came into the world. Through his teaching and healing ministry he invited all the people he met into a deep love attachment to their Creator. He restored the connection that was destroyed through disobedience in the Garden of Eden. His redemptive love displayed through his whole life, culminating with his death on the cross, gave all of humanity a chance to connect to God in the intimate way that God originally intended. The healing accounts record how people made that connection by their willingness to commit to a faith relationship with Jesus and "follow him up the road." They would live in the divine presence forever as they were created to do.

You may recall how the disciples were afraid of following Jesus up that road. Peter tried to offer Jesus an easier way. James and John, just before this story, asked if they could be rewarded and Jesus asked them, *"Can you drink the cup I shall drink or be baptized in the same bath of pain as I?"* They eventually did drink the cup. Here Bartimaeus was ready to follow Jesus anywhere. This account pushes us to reflect on how committed we are to Jesus and his mission. It draws us into a healing relationship with Jesus, which we reaffirm when we share the bread and drink the cup of the Eucharist.

Interestingly, Bartimaeus' name means "son of fear," or filled with fear. After meeting Jesus, there was no sign of fear. He was truly made well. This was more than a physical healing. Bartimaeus was ready to walk up the road with Jesus to Calvary. He became a true disciple and a model for the early Christians and for us. Once Jesus touches our lives and allows us to see with his worldview, we desire to follow him wherever he takes us. We do things we never thought we could do. We stay faithful even in challenging times. Our fears give way to the awesome joy of following in his steps.

Jesus had been on an important mission, but he chose to stop for this man's need. He saw more in Bartimaeus than most people saw. They tried to quiet this man, thinking he was just another blind beggar, but to no avail. Their words were not going to stop this man from meeting Jesus. There was more to this man, and Jesus saw who was under that cloak. He stopped his mission not only to cure but also to make a disciple of the man. The story challenges us to see the core of people and to welcome them on the road to life, the road of following Jesus. Not all will step onto the road, but some will.

For years, I have watched people come to church. Many were searching for something more. It was a great joy to watch them change as they came to know Jesus personally when they opened themselves to the full power of his Holy Spirit. Many had this life-changing experience while going through the Spiritual Enrichment Retreat I mentioned in the introduction. Then, they wanted to serve him. I watched Christian leaders being formed and healed of past hurts and experiencing forgiveness. Once they felt the power of Jesus' healing love and the intimacy they could share with him, they were ready to do whatever he desired. They experienced "attachment love" that involved an intimate, close connection to their Creator. They did things beyond their human capabilities. They served in church leadership, and many became part of my healing teams. They shared the joy of seeing people get well and live a life connected to God.

QUESTIONS TO PONDER/DISCUSS

- When you pray, do you name Jesus and talk to him as a friend?
- What forms of blindness do you feel called to pray for in our world?
- What "cloaks" would you have to throw off to be closer to Jesus?
- What things can we learn from this account for healing ministry?

PRACTICAL APPLICATION

Pray for yourself or others for the courage to follow Jesus wherever he leads you. Pray that you can open your eyes and ears to what Jesus asks of you.

HEALING ACCOUNT 29

Malchus' Ear

READ LUKE 22:47-51 (THIS ACCOUNT IS ALSO FOUND IN MATTHEW 26:50-52; MARK 14:47, AND JOHN 18:10-11, 25-27)

47 While Jesus was still speaking, a crowd came up, and the man who was called Judas, one of the Twelve, was leading them. He approached Jesus to kiss him, 48 but Jesus asked him, "Judas, are you betraying the Son of Man with a kiss?"
49 When Jesus' followers saw what was going to happen, they said, "Lord, should we strike with our swords?" 50 And one of them struck the servant of the high priest, cutting off his right ear.
51 But Jesus answered, "No more of this!" And he touched the man's ear and healed him.

REFLECTION

What is unique about this account is that Jesus offers a gesture of love to an enemy participating in Jesus' death on the cross. He had taught, *"Love your enemies,"* and he demonstrates that message here. He shows compassion and care for a man who would help in his death. Jesus showed divine love toward everyone. He gives a gift to someone who would take his life. His love knew no bounds.

What is also unique about this healing account is that the man did not ask for healing nor did he show any faith in Jesus to heal. In most of the healing stories so far, usually someone asked for a healing, or someone they knew asked. In this case, there is no request or any sense of faith in Jesus. This story demonstrates Jesus' deep divine love and compassion that brought healing. It shows us the core of the healing ministry and informs us about how we can participate in Jesus' ministry. We must be so filled with the love of Jesus that we are ready to reach out and pray for even our enemies. We must be willing to step past human feelings and show Jesus' love to everyone we meet.

This account speaks to situations where people have harmed us, and we are holding unforgiveness in our hearts. We might feel we would never forgive them for their words or actions. In reality, the unforgiveness is keeping us in prison. It is taking its toll on our physical bodies. To set ourselves free, we need to forgive. One way to express our forgiveness is to pray a blessing prayer for them. This may seem difficult, especially if they never apologized, but it is the only way for us to find healing and perhaps bring healing to them. Loving our enemies is a challenge, but by the divine power of Jesus' love, we can do it and bring about healing in his name.

We mentioned at the beginning that to do the ministry of Jesus, we must receive the fullness of God's love for us and be baptized in the power of the Holy Spirit. This is especially true in these kinds of situations. Loving everyone with divine love is possible when we overflow with divine love, which we receive through fully committing to Jesus and accepting his deep love for us.

The early Christians were persecuted and killed for their belief in Jesus. Their friends were killed, yet they had to demonstrate Jesus' love to those who killed them. Christians are facing similar situations in certain places in the world today. This account models a way to love those who do not love us. We each have similar challenging situations in life; therefore, we can find empowerment in this healing story. Jesus lived what he taught and invites us to do the same.

We could ponder why Jesus cured this man. Certainly, it flows from his heart of compassion. He may have also thought this man would change his life and enter into a relationship with him. We have seen how many people, after being cured, made a faith commitment to Jesus. Watching Jesus' unconditional love changed many lives. Even the Centurion who saw the manner of his death said, *"Truly this man was the Son of God"* (Mark 15:39). These demonstrations of divine love are a powerful message to people who watch. This account reminds us that, as Christians, we can change many lives by demonstrating divine love in challenging situations. It is part of bringing healing to our world.

QUESTIONS TO PONDER/DISCUSS

- Do you have any stories of people who brought healing by loving their enemy?
- Why do you think Jesus healed this man's ear?
- Can you share a time when you have been challenged to love your "enemy"?
- What can we take away from this healing account?

PRACTICAL APPLICATION

Take time to bring to mind someone who has been an "enemy" in your life, someone who has hurt you or harmed you. Ask Jesus to bless that person and heal the issue that caused them to harm you. If you are ready, forgive them and continue to pray God's blessings upon them.

The Resurrection of Jesus

READ LUKE 24:1-12 (THIS ACCOUNT IS ALSO FOUND IN MARK 16:1-8, MATTHEW 28:1-10, AND JOHN 20:1-18)

1 On the first day of the week, very early in the morning, the women took spices they had prepared and went to the tomb. 2 They found the stone rolled away from the tomb, 3 but when they entered, they did not find the body of the Lord Jesus. 4 While they were wondering about this, suddenly two men in clothes that gleamed like lightning stood beside them. 5 In their fright the women bowed down with their faces to the ground, but the men said to them, "Why do you look for the living among the dead? 6 He is not here; he has risen! Remember how he told you, while he was still with you in Galilee: 7 'The Son of Man must be delivered into the hands of sinful men, be crucified and on the third day be raised again.'" 8 Then they remembered his words.

9 When they came back from the tomb, they told all these things to the Eleven and to all the others. 10 It was Mary Magdalene, Joanna, Mary the mother of James, and the others with them who told this to the apostles. But they did not believe the women, because their words seemed to them like nonsense. 12 Peter, however, got up and ran to the tomb. Bending over, he saw the strips of linen lying by themselves, and he went away, wondering to himself what had happened.

REFLECTION

There is one miracle that gives meaning to all the rest. It is the resurrection. There is no miracle greater than Jesus' resurrection from the dead. He had raised a number of people during his ministry, and we saw testimonies of people being raised from the dead through prayer, but there is no other story of a person just raised from the dead on their own. No other leader of any religion has ever done that. This miracle clearly proclaims that Jesus was the Son of God and that he was divine. He came forth from the grave on his own divine power flowing from *Abba* through him. This miracle changed all of human history. It lets us to know that God came to this world with a mission to draw people into union with the Trinity. It tells us that Jesus' words were divine, and he wanted us to be well and live with him forever. It gives us the peace of knowing we are forgiven and can share eternal life with him.

When we examine the accounts of the resurrection of Jesus, we notice they vary somewhat, but the stories of his numerous appearances to so many people attest to his living presence after his crucifixion. In his letter to the Corinthians, the apostle Paul recorded that Jesus was seen by Peter and the apostles, and then by more than five hundred people, many of whom were still alive when he wrote that letter.

In addition to the stories of Jesus' living presence, we have the stories of the many changed people. Acts of the Apostles describes how the early Christians continued to feel Jesus' power and do the miracles as he did. The fact that these early followers stayed together and carried on Jesus' ministry attests to his presence in their midst. The first group of one hundred and twenty received his Holy Spirit at Pentecost, and after that, those first Christian, through their baptism, were anointed with the power of that same Holy Spirit. In my book *Healing Miracles in Acts of the Apostles*, I reflected on eighteen of the miracles described in that book. Jesus' presence stayed alive through those people and empowered them to do the things he did. Their deep faith relationship with Jesus allowed them to bring his Presence and personality to the sick, the injured, and the oppressed. When they did, the same type of healings and deliverance occurred.

Early church writers record that the same miracles found in the gospel continued to happen for at least three hundred years. People were baptized as adults and fully committed their lives to Jesus with an openness to the gifts of the Spirit. That power is still available to all who are baptized in the Holy Spirit today. Jesus' resurrection changed the world, and his divine presence continues to change lives. We get to be part of that phenomenal miracle.

SUMMARY

These healing accounts that we have shared demonstrate that Jesus brought the supernatural power of divine love to the world. The power of his love dispelled evil, forgave sins, and healed the sick and wounded. His compassionate heart drew him to reach out to everyone with a desire to make them whole. His words and actions show us that we can receive his love and do what he did in the power of that love. These accounts take us to a new level of understanding life and the eternal possibilities of our lives. They empower us to do the impossible because it is possible in connection to God's love. They demonstrate the treasures of living in a close relationship with Jesus. They give us a picture of God, who is overflowing with love for us. We can only give praise and thanks to be invited into union with this divine love.

This book gives us the initial basis for the healing ministry of Jesus. There is much more to learn. The "Books for Further Reading," plus many others, offer more insights into the healing ministry. For further in-depth training in the healing ministry, see the websites of the places listed at the end of the Appendix. I hope this journey will spark your desire to learn more and to begin practicing this ministry if you have not already done so. It is exciting and a tremendous joy to feel the healing love of God move through us and bring about wholeness in another person. I invite you to step into the journey.

Appendix

WHEN HEALING DOESN'T HAPPEN

Jesus' healing ministry demonstrates that God wants us to be well and whole. We share in Jesus' healing and saving mission because Jesus told us to. He wants his disciples to know him and share in the power of his love. He has commissioned us to pray with others for healing. As we do, we notice that occasionally, a certain healing does not occur when we pray. That can be challenging to understand, but it does not have to stop us from praying. Several factors can hinder healing, and sometimes, we are left with the realization that we are dealing with a mystery. We do not understand each part of this ministry, but we trust that God understands and has a plan for each of us. There is a certain mystery, but we do not have to understand the mystery to do the ministry.

Randy Clark writes, "My obedience to the Great Commission is not conditional on my ability to understand." (This is in a book by Randy Clark and Craig Miller called *Finding Victory When Healing Doesn't Happen*.) We pray for people because Jesus commissioned us to do so, and we know that if we bring the love of Jesus to a person, healing always happens on some level. We pray when we do not understand what the result will be.

Sometimes, people are not healed because of a distorted picture of God. They think that God caused them to be sick or get injured because of something they did wrong. They feel God is against them. God is perfect love and would never cause someone to be sick as a punishment for sin. Evil in the world and people's lack of care for others cause disasters and injury, but the gospels clearly show that God is on the side of healing and wellness. We may have to give people Jesus' picture of God to open them to healing love. The first chapter in my book, *Living a Transformed Life*, offers a picture of God revealed to us by Jesus.

Unforgiveness is probably the biggest hindrance to healing. If we do not forgive someone but hold on to bitterness or a desire for revenge, the love of God cannot come in. Forgiveness is a decision of the will, and by the power of God, we can choose to forgive. We take power away from the person who harmed us and use our power, combined with God's power, to release ourselves from the desire to do equal harm. We can choose to bless them with God's love, which gives us inner freedom and opens the door for healing to happen to us.

Another issue that can hinder healing is not forgiving ourselves. This can be related to a person's strong sense of shame, which makes them feel unworthy of forgiveness. Some significant person early in their life gave the message that they were a mistake or not good enough. It can be a strong voice that keeps them from feeling worthy of God's abundant mercy and healing love. As I ministered to people in the Sacrament of Reconciliation, I found that if I prayed Jesus' forgiveness over a person after they confessed and then prayed for inner healing, they often were able to experience divine love that empowered them to forgive themselves. They felt that they were worthy of forgiveness. This set the stage for greater healing.

As we saw in some of the gospel accounts, there can be a power of evil residing in an inner wound or affecting a person's physical condition. Unaddressed demonic interference can block a person from experiencing healing. Prayer ministers need to be attentive to that possibility. If that is the case, they need to bind the power of the evil spirit and command the evil spirit to leave in Jesus' name. Then, they can pray for inner healing in the place where the spirit had resided.

Appendix

A person has to want to be healed. Sometimes, they may receive a subconscious reward for being ill. They might enjoy the attention or the benefits they receive from their condition. They may not want to change some behavior that contributes to their illness. These things will keep them from getting well.

In the gospel accounts, we saw that Jesus brought divine love to the encounter with a sick or injured person in each healing story. The person he ministered to did not always have faith, but Jesus did. As prayer ministers, we must maintain a deep love connection to Jesus. We must spend time nurturing that relationship so that we have an abundance of divine love to lavish on people who ask for prayer. Our faith connection to Jesus opens the way for that love to flow. We can use simple things like laying on of hands, anointing with oil, and active listening and responding to convey that love. Our expectation of God's love to bring healing can raise the expectation of the person for whom we are praying. Sometimes, we may get a word of knowledge that can open the person to the deeper core issue.

In his book *Breaking Emotional Barriers to Healing*, Craig Miller explains that we may need to go deeper to the core issue when an illness or pain remains. He records many stories of healing after he invited the person to look at possible issues that sat at the core of the wound or condition. Sometimes, this takes more skill than we might have. The stories challenge us to keep learning about Jesus' healing power.

The good news is that whenever we pray in Jesus' name for healing and bring his divine love to a situation, something good, some level of healing always happens. We may not see it immediately, but we know Jesus hears us and wants us to be well. We are privileged to be able to share in this miraculous ministry. We do not set the results. We love with the love of Jesus inside of us. It is a joy to be part of this divine plan.

ACCOUNTS OF JESUS HEALING NUMEROUS PEOPLE

There were many more healings done by Jesus than the ones we have explored. Following are a number of the accounts in which

APPENDIX

he healed numerous people in the crowds. We can stand in those crowds of people and watch him change lives. It is amazing to think of the crowds of people who just wanted to be close to him and feel the anointing of his love. We get to be in those crowds when we quiet ourselves and feel his loving presence swirling around us. We are right there when we pray with people, watch them change, and get healthier.

> Mark 1:32 -35
> 32 That evening after sunset the people brought to Jesus all the sick and demon-possessed. 33 The whole town gathered at the door, 34 and Jesus healed many who had various diseases. He also drove out many demons, but he would not let the demons speak because they knew who he was. 35 Very early in the morning, while it was still dark, Jesus got up, left the house and went off to a solitary place, where he prayed.

> Mark 3:7–10
> 7 Jesus withdrew with his disciples to the lake, and a large crowd from Galilee followed. 8 When they heard all he was doing, many people came to him from Judea, Jerusalem, Idumea, and the regions across the Jordan and around Tyre and Sidon. 9 Because of the crowd, he told his disciples to have a small boat ready for him, to keep people from crowding him. 10 For he had healed many, so that those with diseases were pushing forward to touch him.

> Mark 6:7, 12–13
> 7 Calling the Twelve to him, he sent them out two by two and gave them authority over evil spirits ... 12 They went out and preached that the people should repent. 13 They drove out many demons and anointed many sick people with oil and healed them.

> Mark 6:53–56
> 53 When they had crossed over, they landed at Gennesaret and anchored there. 54 As soon as they got out of the boat, people recognized Jesus. 55 They ran

throughout that whole region and carried the sick on mats to wherever they heard he was. 56 And wherever he went, into villages, towns, or countryside, they placed the sick in the marketplaces. They begged him to let them touch even the edge of his cloak, and all who touched him were healed.

Matthew 11:2-6
2 When John heard in prison what Jesus Christ was doing, he sent his disciples 3 to ask him, "Are you the one who was to come, or should we expect someone else?" 4 Jesus replied, "Go back and report to John what you hear and see: 5 The blind receive sight, the lame walk, those who have leprosy are cured, the deaf hear, the dead are raised, and the good news is preached to the poor. 6 Blessed is the man who does not fall away on account of me."

Matthew 15:29-31
29 Jesus left there and went along the Sea of Galilee. Then he went up on a mountainside and sat down. 30 Great crowds came to him, bringing the lame, the blind, the crippled, the mute and many others, and laid them at his feet; and he healed them. 31 The people were amazed when they saw the mute speaking, the crippled made well, the lame walking and the blind seeing. And they praised the God of Israel.

COMMUNITIES THAT TRAIN AND SUPPORT PEOPLE IN THE HEALING MINISTRY

Christian Healing Ministries at www.christianhealingmin.org
The International Order of St. Luke the Physician at www.osltoday.org
The Association of Christian Therapists at www.actheals.org
OSL South Carolina at osl@oslcharleston.com

About the Author

Rev. Paul has spent his 48 years of priestly ministry passionately leading people in his community and surrounding area to a deep love for God, teaching about the power of God's word, and bringing God's healing touch to many. He has traveled to Australia, Europe, Guatemala, Kenya, Uganda, Madagascar, and nationally, teaching and ministering God's healing love.

Rev. Paul has written eight books:

> *Arise and Walk: The Christian Search for Meaning in Suffering*
> *Paul's Letters for Today's Christian*
> *Journey to Inner Peace*
> *Sacraments: Encountering the Risen Lord*
> *Resting in the Heart*
> *Healing Miracles in Acts of the Apostles*
> *Where Do I Come From? My True Identity*
> *Living a Transformed Life*

In 1979, he became an active member of the Association of Christian Therapists (www.actheals.org). He is now spiritual advisor to that community. In 1996, he became a member of the International Order of St. Luke the Physician (www.osltoday.org), an international organization dedicated to equipping God's people with the healing ministry of Jesus. He has served as president of their board and continues to help lead their ministry. He is also on the National Board of Directors for Christian Healing Ministries (www.christianhealingmin.org), directed by Judith MacNutt.

Rev. Paul retired nine years ago from serving as pastor of St. John's Church and Center for Inner Peace in New London,

About the Author

Wisconsin. He initiated growth in the church by the power of the Holy Spirit to the point where they went from nearly closing to needing a new church building. He designed the new church and was the leading builder for that structure. St. John's was a central place for teaching, worship, and healing ministry for his last 18 years as a pastor.

He has a fire in his heart for inviting people into the heart of God. His gifts of preaching, teaching, praying, and administrating have been anointed by the Holy Spirit to bring many people to greater wholeness and inner peace.

Books for Further Reading

Clark, Randy, and Craig Miller. *Finding Victory When Healing Doesn't Happen.* Pennsylvania: Global Awakening, 2015.
(In this book, one can discover many factors that influence the outcome of healing prayer. It challenges a person to look deeper into an illness or wound to find the core issue that needs to be addressed for the person to get well.)

Feider, Paul. *Healing Miracles in Acts of the Apostles.* Eugene, OR: Wipf & Stock, 2021.
(This book takes the reader into eighteen healing accounts in Acts of the Apostles to discover the power of God's love available to those who commit their lives to Jesus. It has discussion questions for group sharing.)

———. *Living a Transformed Life.* Eugene, OR: Wipf & Stock, 2024.
(This book offers the path to a life of deep peace and joy. It describes how to be transformed with divine energy and divine healing, equipping us to bring hope to the environment in which we live. It includes Jesus' picture of God and his core teachings. It has discussion questions for group sharing.)

———. *Resting in the Heart.* Eugene, OR: Wipf & Stock, 2001.
(This book offers simple, clear steps, along with scriptural reflections, to assist the reader in getting free from childhood memories that stifle their adult life, especially in the areas of fear/anxiety, shame, unresolved grief, and unnamed anger.)

———. *The Journey to Inner Peace.* Eugene, OR: Wipf & Stock, Revised 2015.
(This simple, experiential book offers important steps to true inner peace in Jesus. It speaks of the spiritual base for doing healing ministry. It contains practical application questions and prayers for healing.)

———. *The Spiritual Enrichment Retreat.*
This six-part video series helps participants experience the full release of the Holy Spirit with all the gifts of the Spirit. The meditations for this retreat are found in his book, *Living a Transformed Life.*

Books for Further Reading

———. *Where Do I Come From? My True Identity*. Eugene, OR: Wipf & Stock, 2022.
(What is my true identity? How do I perceive myself? Do I have within me a deep inner joy and peace because of who I am? This unique book takes readers on a profound reflective journey to discover answers to life's most important questions, which readies them for the opportunity to bring peace and healing to others.)

Johnson, Bill. *When Heaven Invades Earth*. Pennsylvania: Destiny Image, 2005.
(A dynamic presentation of how to bring the power of heaven to the world today through the "special forces" given to you by the Holy Spirit.)

Keller, Timothy. *The Reason for God*. New York: Riverhead, 2008.
(The author answers some of the central questions people have about God by presenting a well-thought-out reason for faith in God, who loves deeply. It is an excellent resource for helping people talk about their faith to those who may be skeptical.)

MacNutt, Francis. *Healing*. Indiana: Ave Maria Press, 1999.
(This is one of the first comprehensive books on Jesus' healing ministry and the commission we have to continue his healing work. It is an excellent resource for people learning about the healing ministry.)

———. *The Healing Reawakening*. Michigan: Chosen Books, 2005.
(A unique account of how Jesus' healing ministry has survived through the centuries of Christianity and is viable today.)

MacNutt, Francis, and Judith MacNutt. *Deliverance from Evil Spirits*. Michigan: Chosen Books, 2024.
(This comprehensive, biblically based book equips readers to understand the scriptural basis of deliverance and its relation to inner healing. It is a guide for anyone who meets up with evil in ministry or life.)

MacNutt, Judith. *Angels Are for Real*. Minnesota: Chosen Books, 2012.
(An inspiring book filled with stories of angels and their role in making us aware of the supernatural power available to us.)

Miller, Craig. *Breaking Emotional Barriers to Healing*. Pennsylvania: Whitaker House, 2018.
(The author offers profound insight into the connection between wounded emotions and physical illness. He offers methods to release the underlying emotions and bring physical healing.)

Montague, George. *Mark: Good News for Hard Times*. Michigan: Servant Books, 1981.
(In this book, the author gives sound background information on the gospel of Mark, which makes that gospel more understandable and enlightening.)

Moreland, J.P. *Love Your God with All Your Mind*. Colorado Springs: NavPress, 2012.
(Moreland makes a compelling case for Christians to use their God-given intellect to help in their spiritual development and enable them to bring others to believe in Jesus.)

Books for Further Reading

———. *A Simple Guide to Experience Miracles.* Michigan: Zondervan, 2021.

(This book contains accounts of numerous, inspiring, present-day healings and offers ways of connecting with God to make these events happen in our lives.)

Rice, John. *Called to Bless—Restoring God's Ministry of Blessing.* Eugene, OR: Wipf & Stock, 2024.

(This book focuses on God's promise to bless and our calling to bless one another. Many blessing stories are interspersed, revealing how God's goodness and grace are released when we speak words of blessing wherever needed.)

www.ingramcontent.com/pod-product-compliance
Lightning Source LLC
Chambersburg PA
CBHW070919180426
43192CB00038B/1860